Other books by Martha Watson Murphy

How to Start and Operate Your Own Bed-and-Breakfast

The Bed & Breakfast Cookbook

A New England
Fish Tale

Seafood Recipes

and

Observations of a Way of Life

from

a Fisherman's Wife

MARTHA WATSON MURPHY

❧ *A New England* ❧
FISH TALE

Henry Holt and Company
New York

Henry Holt and Company, Inc.
Publishers since 1866
115 West 18th Street
New York, New York 10011

Henry Holt® is a registered
trademark of Henry Holt and Company, Inc.

Published in Canada by Fitzhenry & Whiteside Ltd.,
195 Allstate Parkway, Markham, Ontario L3R 4T8.

Library of Congress Cataloging-in-Publication Data
Murphy, Martha W.
A New England fish tale: seafood recipes and
observations of a way of life from a
fisherman's wife / Martha Watson Murphy. — 1st ed.
p.   cm.
Includes index.
1. Cookery (Fish)   2. Cookery (Seafood)   I. Title.
TX747.M874   1997   96-44778
641.6'92—dc20   CIP

ISBN 0-8050-4204-0

Henry Holt books are available for special promotions
and premiums. For details contact: Director, Special Markets.

First Edition—1997

DESIGNED BY BETTY LEW

Printed in the United States of America
All first editions are printed on acid-free paper. ∞

1   3   5   7   9   10   8   6   4   2

Overleaf: Coming through the "gap" at Galilee, a lobster boat
makes its way home and a dragger heads out to sea.

I suppose everyone is partial to the port they consider their own, and I'm no exception. For me, there has always been something special about the port of Galilee in Narragansett, Rhode Island. Bathed in the washed light reflected back from the water that nearly surrounds the port, the air here has a luminous quality. That light and the separateness of this place create a sense of ease that seems to hang in the air.

To

Kevin Ian Murphy

and

all the others

who go down to the sea in ships

They that go down to the sea in ships, that do business

in great waters: These see the works of the Lord,

and his wonders in the deep.

—Psalm 107

Acknowledgments

There are lots of people to thank for helping make this book a reality, and it's with great pleasure that I acknowledge them.

For her unending enthusiasm for this book, I thank my agent, Susan P. Urstadt.

For her patience and miraculous editing, many thanks to Beth Crossman.

For helping me test and develop recipes, and keeping an even temperament through it all, I thank Dwayne Ridgaway.

For generously and graciously sharing their stories I thank the women of the Gloucester Fishermen's Wives association: Sefatia Romeo, Lena Novello, Josephine Russo, and Grace Favazza, in particular; and Pat Percy of the Portland Fishermen's Wives association, along with Carrie Suchar, Gail Johnson, and Jeanette Bubar.

For statistics, Ralph Boragine of the Rhode Island Seafood Council has been a tireless source.

My thanks to the Women's Fisheries Network for their interest and help, and special thanks to Madeleine Hall-Arber for sharing her research on commercial fishermen and their families.

The photographs in this book tell the story in a way that words alone cannot. For them and for some of the other bits of information about fishing in New England, I thank the following for their help: Martha Towne; Herman Lippman; Ellen Nelson of the Cape Ann Historical Society; Dan Buckley of the Chatham

Historical Society; Gerald Abbott and Lisa Nolan of the Block Island Historical Society; Phil Budlong of the Mystic Seaport Museum; Bill Ostendorf of the *Providence Journal*; the *New Bedford Standard Times* and Jack Iddon; the Historical Society of Stonington, Connecticut; and Brenda Figuerido of the National Marine Fisheries Service at Woods Hole Oceanographic Institute.

Thanks to my entire family for their encouragement, and particular thanks to my parents, Bob and Nancy Watson, for their long-ago lessons. They were my first and best teachers in the kitchen, and everywhere else in life, for that matter. They introduced me and my brother and sisters at early ages to everything from oysters on the half-shell to fried green tomatoes, cheese soufflés, and live lobsters. Along the way they taught me that the world is wide and varied, and as I progress in my own travels upon it, their influence is with me every day.

Lastly, and with deep affection, thanks to Kevin, and to all my other fishing friends, for giving me something to write about.

Contents

Hauling in the net aboard the F/V Eleanor, *owned by Ellery Thompson.*
Probably off Stonington, Connecticut, about 1945.

"We used to haul in by hand. If you had 10,000 pounds of butterfish, you'd haul until you couldn't haul no more, and then the boat would roll and you'd pinch it against the rails and pull it up some more when the boat rolled back. Then when you'd get to the cod end, we'd hook the whip to it and lift it in. Four guys could pull in a net of 10,000 pounds. I wouldn't still be fishing without net drums. People used to retire in their fifties unless they were the captain."

—a fisherman from Narragansett, Rhode Island

Introduction

When I meet someone for the first time, sooner or later the conversation turns to the subject of our spouses. The revelation that my husband is a commercial fisherman almost invariably draws a look of surprise if not a stunned silence. But in my heart of hearts I'm as surprised as anyone to find myself married to a fisherman. After all, commercial fishing is a world of manual labor and macho men, big on brawn and short on brains, isn't it? Why would I want to have anything to do with it?

The stereotypes are partly true—this *is* a place for macho men and misfits (terms I use with complete affection), and anyone who wants to hide out from society at large. But behind the stereotypes exists a world of complexity, sophistication, and contradictions, and a history that is rich and old. As I was to learn, all sorts of talented, intelligent men and women have been seduced by commercial fishing—men and women who could do any number of other things for a living but who have, for various reasons, chosen this backbreaking, risky line of work.

Most of us don't get to meet these people or see their world because it is hidden. The work itself takes place on a "foreign" element—the water—while the rest of us spend our days on firm ground. That and a schedule unlike any other combine to keep commercial fishermen and their way of earning a living a mystery.

I was introduced to this hidden world more than a dozen years ago when I started dating the man who would later become my husband. Along the way I fell in love with the life itself. It's hard not to if you spend time around the boats, the people, and the ports. And for some time I've wanted to tell part of their story. It seemed only natural to do so along with a collection of seafood recipes, for it is *food*, after all, that they provide to us.

What attracts young men and women to fishing? Certainly the physical environment is part of it; that is always mentioned when fishermen are asked what they like about their jobs. Harbors, sounds, and the open ocean are pretty unbeatable places to spend time unless the weather is bad, but even then there is the thrill of being out in it all and making it back home safely.

There is an element of clarity about fishing that can be immensely appealing: Things on a boat have to work properly and well, and they either do or they don't; there is no middle ground.

Fishing also offers a way to "get away from it all"—the rest of us and the petty hassles of everyday life ashore, that is—and I think a lot of people who fish for a living, whether they've thought about it or not, have chosen fishing, at least partially, for this reason. One of the trade-offs is a schedule that is nearly completely unpredictable from day to day, making it hard to find loved ones who will put up with that part of the bargain. But as I can attest, loved ones do put up with it, and find ways to weave a life around this unusual occupation.

The two other most frequently mentioned reasons for wanting to go fishing are being one's own boss (even crew are "self-employed") and the satisfaction that comes from meeting the challenges of the job. Certainly most of us can understand the appeal of independence, but it has a cost: Fishermen have no guaranteed income. And the challenges that fishermen love meeting would drive most people crazy: working in an environment that is dangerous and unpredictable, and figuring out how to bring back seafood that remains hidden from view until the net or trap is aboard—and for prices that fluctuate as wildly as the stock market. Surviving and thriving in this business requires physical strength and mental acuity in equal measures.

These common threads—a love of the sea, an independent spirit, and an enjoyment of hard work—connect fishermen as a group, despite differences in background and education.

Any examination of commercial fishing in New England today leads to its past. I was interested to find, for example, that commercial fishing was of crucial economic importance to the early colonists and a pivotal factor in the Revolutionary War. By the late nineteenth century the fishing schooners of

Gloucester, Massachusetts, made up the most successful fishing fleet in the world. And today the state of Maine is still the nation's largest supplier of fresh lobster.

The history is interesting, but what consistently struck me as I did research for this book were the men and women who have inhabited it. Their faces and voices, captured in photographs and in books, reveal inquisitive spirits, souls readily awed by the natural world, and lives led with quiet bravery. Small glimpses of their stories are presented throughout this book.

This account would not be complete without mentioning some of the crises faced by New England fishermen today. There is disagreement between fishermen and scientists as to whether certain species have been "overfished" or not, and there is great disagreement between fishermen and the government on how to address the problems. Some fishermen do not admit to any serious changes in the stocks at all, saying that fish populations are cyclical, while others who do admit declines in populations blame them on pollution or fisheries other than the one in which they participate: Gillnetters blame draggermen, draggermen blame gillnetters, and round and round it goes.

It is not my purpose in this book to take a stand on the issues of fishing and government regulations. It is my belief that fishermen will find a way through this crisis and that commercial fishing will remain a viable and beautiful way of life for as long as we have oceans and the hardy souls eager to venture out on them.

The recipes here are meant to encourage you to try a variety of seafood in a variety of ways. Many, if not most, of these recipes are my own invention (I am lucky to have a husband who brings home a steady supply of various seafood); then there are recipes I've adapted from other sources over the years, and those that are credited directly to the originator. The old saying "There is nothing new under the sun" is true, especially when it comes to recipes, but I hope you'll find a collection here that *is* new to you, and one you'll turn to again and again. I am confident that you can reproduce these dishes well in your own kitchen.

Primarily, I hope this book will provide you with a look inside the world of commercial fishing—who the fishermen are and how the fish on your table are caught, as well as new ideas for preparing seafood dishes and reasons to add more seafood to your diet. And I hope it will give you a new respect for the men and women who go down to the sea in ships. This book is my tribute to them— the ones out there today and all who have gone before.

1

Starters

Old salt in oilers, Gloucester, Massachusetts, the early 1900s.

"From the time of the earliest English seasonal fishing camps in New England, the men who caught fish were a 'peripheral' group in society. The early settlers of the Plymouth and Massachusetts Bay Colonies hired itinerant fishermen, many of whom were from a large pool of maritime laborers, and few of whom embraced Puritanism. . . . The nature of fishing itself mitigated against its respectability as a Puritan calling; it was seasonal, market-oriented work, and by its nature at odds with the Puritan belief that 'work was pleasing to God only when performed in a regular and disciplined manner.' "
—Daniel Vickers, cited in Sandra Oliver, *Saltwater Foodways*

Gravlax with Mustard Dill Sauce

Smoked Bluefish Pâté

Johnnycakes with Smoked Mackerel and Caramelized Apples

Smoked Salmon with Herbed Goat Cheese

Squid Rings with Red Pepper Coulis

Black Bean Nachos with Lobster Salsa

Mussel-Filled Focaccia

Crab and Roasted Red Pepper Dip

Johnnycakes

Seafood-Stuffed Focaccia

This chapter contains eight diverse recipes for using seafood as an hors d'oeuvre or party food. They will allow you to offer your guests a small portion of something special and delicious before dinner. Or in larger portions along with numerous other choices, they can supply the entire evening's menu.

Most of the dishes can be made in advance, always a plus for a host. You will find recipes that call for inexpensive, commonly available New England seafood, such as mussels and squid, as well as those that include the more expensive delicacies, such as lobster and smoked salmon. And you will consistently find a heavy reliance on *fresh* herbs—dried simply will not give you the same results. There is something here for every season and every pocketbook. Mostly I hope you'll find recipes that you'll love and that are new to you.

Don't consider these recipes the beginning and end of hors d'oeuvre ideas, however. Many other suitable first-course dishes are tucked into the chapters that follow.

Broiled or grilled oysters, littleneck clams, or mussels in the shell make lovely hors d'oeuvres; directions for preparing them can be found at the beginning of the Main Course—Shellfish chapter. Simply serve with lemon wedges, chilled cocktail sauce, or homemade herbed mayonnaise.

GRAVLAX WITH MUSTARD DILL SAUCE

Gravlax is fish that has been cured with a salt and sugar mixture; salmon is a perfect candidate for this treatment, as is any other high-fat fish. The process allows the meat to stay moist and full, unlike smoking, which dries the fish and shrinks it in the process. This is an old Scandinavian technique, and remarkably easy. The fish will take about four days to cure and then may be kept in the refrigerator for up to two weeks.

In Norway, gravlax is on the breakfast menu, but in the United States it is served as an hors d'oeuvre with crackers or thin slices of rye or pumpernickel bread, lightly buttered. Wedges of fresh lemon and lime or Mustard Dill Sauce is the only accompaniment needed. Chilled aquavit makes a traditional and delicious aperitif.

Serves 8 to 10

> ¼ *cup kosher salt*
> ¼ *cup sugar*
> 2 *tablespoons freshly ground black pepper*
> 3 *tablespoons chopped fresh dill*
> *Two 1-pound salmon fillets, with scaled skin left on*

✻ In a small bowl combine the salt, sugar, pepper, and dill.

✻ Place one fillet, skin side down, in a 9-inch by 13-inch glass dish. Sprinkle the salt/sugar mixture evenly over the fish. Lay the other fillet over this, skin side up, with the thick end of the upper fillet placed over the thin end of the bottom fillet.

✻ Cover the dish with plastic wrap and then foil. Place a pan or tray equal to the length of the fillets on top, then add a 5-pound weight (such as a bag of flour or sugar). Refrigerate.

✻ Twice every 24 hours for the next 3 days, flip the fillets and baste them with the liquid that has formed in the pan; also baste between the fillets. Replace the plastic wrap, foil, and 5-pound weight, and return dish to the refrigerator. On the fourth day, scrape off and discard any salt mixture remaining on the fish. Rinse quickly with fresh cold water; pat dry. The salmon is now ready to slice and serve.

To slice:

Place the salmon on a cutting board, skin side down, and slice very thinly holding the knife at a slight angle. As the knife hits the skin, give it a little sideways push and the meat will slide off the skin.

MUSTARD DILL SAUCE

Makes about ½ cup

3½ tablespoons Dijon mustard   1½ tablespoons fresh lemon juice
1 teaspoon dry mustard   ⅓ cup vegetable oil
2½ tablespoons sugar   3 tablespoons chopped fresh dill

Unloading redfish—Rockport, Massachusettes, 1945.

Unloading the catch is still a manual job. Men in the hold, called "lumpers," send baskets of fish up to be swung off the boat to men on the pier who transport it to the buyer or processing house.

✄   In a blender combine the mustards, sugar, and lemon juice. Slowly add the oil, blending to form a thick mixture. When all the oil is added and the mixture is the desired thickness, transfer it to a bowl and stir in the dill by hand. Cover and refrigerate until ready to use.

Note: We have found that gravlax can take the place of Canadian bacon to make eggs Benedict, topped with a lemony, dill-flavored hollandaise sauce.

SMOKED BLUEFISH PÂTÉ

Smoked fish makes a great hors d'oeuvre on its own, but for variety it is also wonderful made up as a pâté. Here, smoked bluefish is paired with carmelized onions and mushrooms, herbs, brandy, and goat cheese. This is flavorful and rich, and spreads well on rye toasts or crackers—a great start to an evening or to take along on a special picnic. May be made a day in advance.

Makes about 2 cups of pâté

1 tablespoon oil	*1 bay leaf*
1 tablespoon butter	*3 juniper berries, crushed (optional)*
¼ cup chopped onion	*¼ cup brandy*
1 cup sliced mushrooms	*½ pound smoked bluefish*
2 peppercorns	*5 ounces goat cheese*
1 whole clove	*2 tablespoons light cream*

✄   In a large, heavy skillet heat the oil and butter over medium heat. Add the onion, mushrooms, and spices, and cook, stirring occasionally, until the vegetables are tender and have golden brown edges. Pour in the brandy and continue to cook until the liquid has reduced by half. Remove from the heat, and when cool enough to touch, remove and discard the bay leaf and clove.

Place the vegetable mixture in the bowl of a food processor. Pull the skin off the bluefish and add it in chunks to the vegetables. Add the cheese, in bits, and the light cream. Pulse to blend completely, scraping down the side of the bowl with a spatula a couple of times. When the mixture is smooth, transfer it to a small, covered terrine. Chill for at least 1 hour before serving.

Note: For a chunky pâté, reserve some of the carmelized vegetables to stir into the pâté after it has been blended.

If you can't find juniper berries, make the pâté without them. It will still be delicious.

Johnnycakes

Johnnycakes are thin, small pancakes made from stone-ground white cornmeal. They were popular during colonial times and across the frontier long after independence, but they are still considered by most to be one of the quintessential traditional foods of New England.

The name, spelled with or without the "h," is an odd one, and arguments persist about its original meaning. Some scholars claim that the name is a misspelling of the word "journey" (which the colonists would have pronounced much the way we say "johnny") and that the little pancakes were called that because they traveled well. I don't quite buy this; a day-old johnnycake that has been riding around in your pocket is in a lot worse shape than a day-old biscuit or piece of hardtack. Other food historians say the word "journey" was commonly used then as "day" or "by the day," as with "journeyman," a laborer hired and paid by the day. This makes more sense to me. These "cakes" (as many little pan-cooked quick breads were then called) could be speedily and economically made fresh each day, unlike yeasted loaf bread, and thus it is easily conceivable that they were referred to, in the vernacular of the day, as "johnnycakes."

JOHNNYCAKES WITH SMOKED MACKEREL AND CARAMELIZED APPLES

A crisp, thin johnnycake the size of a silver dollar is topped with slices of apples, which have been sautéed with a little maple syrup, and then with a piece of smoked mackerel—the perfect hors d'oeuvre for a fall party and one that showcases some of the best of New England's products.

For this recipe the batter is made very thin so that the johnnycakes are thinner and crisper than usual.

Makes 18

For the johnnycakes:

> *½ cup johnnycake meal*
> *(stone-ground white cornmeal)*
> *½ cup scalded milk*
> *½ cup boiling water*
> *Pinch of salt and pepper*

For the apples:

> *1½ tablespoons butter*
> *2 Granny Smith apples, peeled, cored,*
> *and cut in ¼-inch sections (about 2 cups)*
> *1 tablespoon maple syrup*

Fish:

> *¼ to ½ pound smoked mackerel, sliced in*
> *¼-inch sections off the skin*

To make the johnnycakes:

≫ In a large bowl mix together the johnnycake meal, milk, boiling water, salt, and pepper. Drop a tablespoon of batter onto a lightly oiled hot griddle or skillet. It should spread out to a thin silver-dollar size. If it runs out larger and separates like lace cookies, the batter is too thin; thicken with cornmeal. If the batter holds its shape and does not spread out, thin it with a little hot water. Keep the skillet or griddle lightly oiled while cooking the johnnycakes.

≫ Allow the johnnycakes to cook for about 3 minutes before turning; the bottom should be golden. Cook the other side until golden and transfer immediately to a cooling rack so that the johnnycakes can become crisp.

To caramelize the apples:

≫ Place the butter in a large, heavy skillet over medium heat. When it is hot, add the apples without crowding them and cook, turning with a spatula, until light golden on both sides. Add the maple syrup to the pan and continue cooking until the apples turn a darker golden color. This will not take long—do not allow the apples to become mushy! When done they should be firm but tender and a beautiful golden color. Transfer to a plate to cool.

To assemble the hors d'oeuvres:

≫ Place the thoroughly cooled johnnycakes on a serving platter. Top each with about 3 apple slices, attractively fanned, and over that place a slice or two of smoked mackerel. Add to the platter a few lemon wedges, sprigs of fresh sage, and a small pot of mustard seasoned with finely chopped fresh sage. Serve immediately.

Caring for a Resource

It seems concerns regarding overfishing have been with us a long time. In 1652 the Puritan legislators decreed that codfish, haddock, hake, and pollack could not be taken during the winter months because that was their time for spawning.

SMOKED SALMON WITH HERBED GOAT CHEESE

Since buying smoked salmon requires hardly any effort on your part, the little time you'll spend making the herbed goat cheese will be well worth it. And that is just about all the work there is to making these little toasted slices of baguette spread with goat cheese and fresh herbs, topped with cucumber, smoked salmon, more fresh dill, and lots of fresh lemon juice. *Serves 10*

For the goat cheese spread:

10 ounces goat cheese

2 tablespoons softened butter

2 tablespoons finely chopped flat-leaf parsley

2 tablespoons finely chopped scallions

1 tablespoon chopped fresh dill

½ teaspoon freshly ground black pepper

For the toasts:

1 loaf of French bread, thinly sliced

2–3 tablespoons olive oil

1½ pounds smoked salmon

1 cucumber, peeled and thinly sliced

1 bunch of fresh dill

2 lemons, cut in wedges

To make the goat cheese spread:

In a medium bowl combine all the ingredients well with a fork. Cover and refrigerate until ready to use.

To make the toasts:

Slice the French bread in generous ¼-inch slices. Brush both sides with a little oil and place under the broiler. Toast each side until golden. Transfer to a rack to cool completely.

To assemble the hors d'oeuvres:

Spread each cooled toast with some of the goat cheese mixture. Place a paper-thin slice of cucumber on the goat cheese and top it with a thin slice of smoked salmon. Place a small sprig of dill on the salmon and then squeeze lemon juice over all. Serve immediately.

SQUID RINGS WITH RED PEPPER COULIS

If you've had fried squid rings in restaurants and been disappointed with the rubbery texture and lack of flavor, this recipe will present you with a completely different experience. Squid is delicate, tender, and sweet, and instead of masking its flavor with hot pepper salsa, it is enhanced with the sweet, smoky flavor of roasted red bell peppers. The squid can be fried or baked.

Serves 6 to 8

For the coulis:

5 or 6 large red bell peppers, roasted, peeled with liquid reserved (see page 209)

1 tablespoon olive oil

1 tablespoon butter

1½ cups diced onions

3 cloves garlic, thinly sliced

1 cup dry white wine

1 tablespoon fresh lemon juice

2 tablespoons finely chopped fresh parsley

For the squid rings:

2½ pounds medium-size squid

2½ cups unbleached flour

1 teaspoon salt

1 teaspoon freshly ground black pepper

¼ teaspoon paprika

3 eggs

½ to ¾ cup vegetable oil

To make the coulis:

⋙ Chop the peppers.

⋙ In a large, heavy skillet heat the oil and butter over medium heat. Add the onions and garlic, and cook until tender but not browned. Add the chopped peppers (you should have about 3 cups) and continue cooking over medium-low heat, stirring occasionally, until the mixture is tender. Add the wine and cook until the liquid is reduced by half. Remove from the heat.

⋙ Reserve half of the pepper and onion mixture in a large bowl. Transfer the remainder to a food processor and process into a puree. Add the pureed mix to the mixture in the bowl. Stir in the lemon juice, parsley, and any reserved juices from the roasted peppers.

To make fried squid rings:

✍ For directions on cleaning squid, see page 25. Slice the cleaned squid bodies into ¼-inch rings. Leave the tentacles in whole clusters or separate into individual pieces.

✍ Combine the flour, salt, pepper, and paprika in a large bowl. In a separate bowl beat the eggs.

✍ Dredge the squid in the flour, dip in the egg, and then in the flour again. Repeat until all the squid has been coated.

✍ In a large skillet heat the oil over medium heat (the skillet should have oil at a depth of ½ inch). When it is hot but not smoking, add as many of the squid rings and tentacles as will fit without crowding. Cook over medium heat, turning with tongs, until golden on all sides. When done transfer to a plate lined with brown paper and place in a warm oven. The squid will cook quickly—in about 2 minutes—and should be allowed to sit at room temperature for a minute before serving. Serve with warm or room-temperature red pepper coulis and lemon wedges.

To bake squid rings:

✍ Coat the squid rings with seasoned dried bread crumbs. Arrange in a single layer on a lightly oiled cookie sheet. Drizzle with a little olive oil and bake at 450 degrees for about 10 minutes.

BLACK BEAN NACHOS WITH LOBSTER SALSA

This is a knockout nacho! White corn chips are topped with black bean paste and cheddar cheese, broiled, and then topped with a salsa that is chock-full of lobster, avocado, tomato, and cilantro. This recipe requires only a scant half pound of lobster meat, but your guests will think you've gone all out for them. Great with margaritas!

The salsa needs to chill for one hour before serving.

Makes 24 nachos

For the salsa:

⅓ cup chopped scallions　　　　　*1 tablespoon chopped fresh cilantro*
1 cup seeded and chopped tomatoes　　*⅛ teaspoon salt*
1 clove garlic, minced　　　　　　*½ pound cooked lobster meat, chopped*
1 tablespoon balsamic vinegar　　　*1 avocado, chopped*
3 tablespoons fresh lime juice　　　*¼ teaspoon minced green chile pepper*

For the bean paste:

1 cup cooked and drained black beans
1 tablespoon sour cream
Salt and pepper to taste

24 large white corn tortilla chips
½ pound cheddar cheese, grated

To make the salsa:

Combine all the salsa ingredients in a large bowl and toss. Cover and refrigerate for 1 hour to allow flavors to develop.

To make the bean paste:

Using a food processor or blender, combine the beans with the sour cream; puree to desired consistency. Add salt and pepper to taste. Set aside.

To assemble the nachos:

Preheat the broiler. Place the corn chips on a large cookie sheet. Spread about a teaspoon of bean paste on each chip. Sprinkle a little grated cheese on top of the bean paste. Place under the broiler for approximately 1 minute, or until the cheese is melted. Transfer to a platter and top each nacho with a generous teaspoon of lobster salsa. Serve immediately.

Variation:

Top the corn chip with bean paste, grated cheese, and a marinated small shrimp (shelled and deveined). Place under the broiler until the shrimp is pink. Serve with a tomato salsa.

MUSSEL-FILLED FOCACCIA

Focaccia is that wonderful flat Italian bread, usually flavored with fresh rosemary and olive oil. Here a savory mixture of mussels and vegetables is spread between two layers of classic focaccia dough, the top layer is oiled and sprinkled with salt and rosemary in the traditional way, and then the whole is baked until it is golden. When done, the warm, moist filling sits neatly between fragrant yeasty layers of bread—a perfect hors d'oeuvre or picnic fare.

Makes one 9-inch round focaccia

Filling:

2 dozen live mussels (with shells of 2–2½ inches), cleaned, steamed, and with 2 tablespoons of cooking liquid reserved (page 142)

2 tablespoons olive oil

1 cup chopped plum tomatoes

½ cup chopped green bell pepper

2 cloves garlic, chopped

¼ cup chopped onion

2 tablespoons sweet vermouth

1 teaspoon chopped fresh rosemary

1 teaspoon chopped fresh oregano or marjoram

Salt and pepper to taste

⅓ portion of basic focaccia dough (page 200)

Topping:

1 tablespoon olive oil

¼ teaspoon kosher salt

1 tablespoon fresh rosemary

To make the filling:

✥ Pick the mussels from the shells. While doing this, feel for and remove any grit or beard that you may have missed when you cleaned the mussels. Set the mussels in a bowl and cover.

✥ Heat the olive oil in a large, heavy skillet over medium heat. Add the tomatoes and cook for about 4 minutes. Add the bell pepper, garlic, and onion, and continue cooking until the pepper and onion are tender. Add the vermouth and mussel liquid, stir, and add the herbs, salt, and pepper. Continue cooking over a gentle heat until most of the liquid has evaporated. Remove from the heat and add the mussels.

To assemble the focaccia:

⋙ Take half of the focaccia dough and form it into a ball. Flatten it with your hand and place it in an ungreased 9-inch round cake pan. Using your hands, push and shape the dough to cover the bottom of the pan and halfway up the sides. Using a pastry brush, apply water to a 1-inch band on the outer edge of the dough.

⋙ Spread the mussel mixture evenly over the dough, up to the moistened 1-inch band.

⋙ Roll out the remaining half of the focaccia dough to a thickness of approximately ¼ inch to ½ inch. Drape this over the filling and pinch the top layer of dough to the moistened band on the bottom layer.

⋙ Preheat oven to 400 degrees.

⋙ Brush the dough with the olive oil, sprinkle with salt and rosemary, and bake for 40 minutes. Remove to a rack and cool slightly before slicing.

Heading out for the day, Point Judith, Rhode Island, 1940s.

When fishermen are asked what they like about fishing, they always mention the physical beauty of the ocean and the opportunity to be out on it for long silent stretches, and "doing what I want, when I want, and how I want."

Seafood-Stuffed Focaccia

There are many seafood filling possibilities for focaccia. Consider combining chopped seared scallops with spinach and leeks, or anchovy fillets with black olives and onions.

Focaccia dough can be refrigerated, and if you make the basic recipe and want to make only one seafood focaccia, you will have enough dough left over for two more at another time. Wrap the dough in a clean, damp linen dish towel and then wrap that tightly in plastic wrap. It can be kept in the refrigerator for up to three days.

Focaccia is traditionally brushed with oil and sprinkled with salt and fresh rosemary before baking. If you prefer, you can knead the rosemary into the dough that will be the top crust; the rosemary sprinkled over the focaccia before baking looks pretty but tends to fall off as the focaccia is sliced. As a variation, pressed garlic can also be rubbed into the top of the focaccia before oiling and salting.

The shape of the finished focaccia can be round or oblong; cut into wedges or sliced in strips, this makes a fabulous hors d'oeuvre served hot or at room temperature — or make some a day ahead for a perfect picnic item.

CRAB AND ROASTED RED PEPPER DIP

This makes a great dip for cold artichokes or piled into a ripe avocado or atop bruschetta spread with Herbed Goat Cheese (page 10). Try it once and you'll find many more uses for it.

Makes about 3 cups

½ *pound cooked lump crabmeat*
2 *cups sour cream*
1 *red bell pepper, roasted, skin and*
    seeds removed, and chopped
    (about ⅔ cup) (see page 209)

2 *tablespoons chopped fresh basil*
1 *clove garlic, pressed*
¼ *cup chopped scallion*
Salt and pepper to taste

✎ Combine all ingredients well in a large bowl. Cover and refrigerate for at least 1 hour before using to allow flavors to develop. Remove from refrigerator 10 minutes before using so that the mixture is not ice cold.

Preparing trawls for the dories, aboard a Gloucester schooner, around 1920.

In the last part of the nineteenth century, dory trawling (for cod and halibut) and purse seining (for mackerel) replaced "jigging" over a ship's rail. These new techniques radically transformed commercial fishing; landings were hugely increased, as was the risk for the men. Once the schooner was on the fishing grounds, the dories would be launched, with two men in each, and would regularly travel a mile or two from the ship to set baited trawl lines. Fog, changes in the weather, and the risk of capsizing were constant hazards.

Pizzas

2

The fishing schooner Gertrude L. Thebaud *on a starboard tack, 1920s.*

In the days of schooner fishing, fishermen were not lost only when a ship went down. Some of the dorymen never made it back to the ship; some fell out of the rigging, were struck by booms, or were washed overboard by high seas.

Pizza, as it turns out, is not "junk food" after all. A wholesome crust topped with fresh herbs and vegetables and a little meat and cheese is a healthy meal. Pizza can be low in fat, high in fiber, and relatively low in calories; add a crisp green salad, and you have dinner. Cut into small squares or triangles, these pizzas also make fabulous hors d'oeuvres.

The five recipes here will show you how to make healthful, delicious pizzas using seafood as the meat—a topping that has been largely overlooked.

To keep things simple, you can buy pizza dough at the supermarket (it's usually packaged in bags and kept in the dairy section). Or you can make your own, with the Basic Pizza Dough recipe on page 24.

The possibilities for seafood pizzas are far greater than the handful of recipes given here. How about lump crabmeat with fresh corn kernels and Fontina cheese? Or smoked mackerel with apples and Gorgonzola? You will soon come up with your own combinations.

Boston fish pier, 1950s.

In the old Massachusetts State House on Boston's Beacon Hill, an imposing wooden codfish hangs above the public gallery balcony in the chamber of the House of Representatives. Almost five feet in length, the carving was presented to the legislature in 1784 by a merchant named Jonathan Rowe to remind the members of the importance of the codfishing industry. Today it serves as a reminder to us all of that history and the role fishing has played in establishing Boston as a major New England city and port.

Making Pizza Dough

When making pizza dough, you can mix the ingredients by hand in a large bowl or with a food processor. Either way, there is a little kneading required before letting the dough rise. It needs to rise for one hour but may then be refrigerated until you are ready to use it. Pizza dough will keep in the refrigerator for at least a week, so make a double batch and store half for later use.

Shaping Pizza Dough

Pizzas can be round or rectangular. Place the dough on a board sprinkled with a little flour. Using your hands or a rolling pin, flatten the ball of dough. Flour your hands or the rolling pin and, starting in the center of the dough, push down and out. It will be springy and will tend to pull back into a smaller shape than you've made. Once you have the dough in the shape and thickness you want, let it sit for fifteen minutes. Then, if necessary, shape the dough again before topping.

Using a Pizza Stone

You can use a pizza stone, pizza pan, cookie sheet, or jelly roll pan when making pizza. Experiment and see which you prefer. If you are using a metal pan, always give it a thin wipe of olive oil and then a sprinkle of cornmeal before laying the crust on it. With a stone, just a sprinkle of cornmeal is necessary to keep the dough from sticking and to produce a crispy crust.

BASIC PIZZA DOUGH

Makes enough for one 12-inch to 14-inch round pizza

1 package dry yeast (2½ teaspoons)   *2 tablespoons olive oil*
½ teaspoon sugar   *2 cups unbleached white flour*
⅔ cup warm water   *½ teaspoon salt*

Place the yeast, sugar, and ⅓ cup of warm water in a large bowl and stir to dissolve. Let sit for 10 minutes. Add the remaining ⅓ cup of water, olive oil, flour, and salt, and blend well. Form the dough into a ball, place on a floured board, and knead until smooth and elastic — 5 to 10 minutes.

A grandfather pitches in mending traps.

Fishing in New England has more often than not been a family endeavor. Even when an older member is no longer able to go out on the boats, he can play an important role shoreside — repairing gear, buying supplies, and seeing to the many other details required in the business. This support can help the younger generation tremendously, allowing them to focus more on the actual work of fishing itself.

✍ Form into a ball and place the dough in a large lightly oiled bowl. Turn the dough once so that it is lightly oiled on all sides. Cover the bowl with a clean dish towel and leave in a warm place for 1 hour. The dough should double in size. Punch it down and either roll it out on a lightly floured board to use immediately or wrap well in plastic wrap and refrigerate until ready to use.

✍ You can add chopped fresh herbs, pressed garlic, or grated Parmesan cheese to the pizza dough.

How to Clean Squid

You can buy cleaned squid (fresh or frozen) at the fish market to save a little time in the kitchen. But you'll pay for this convenience—about three times as much as fresh whole squid. Cleaning squid is easy, and fresh squid is tastier and more tender than frozen. Follow these steps:

1. *Remove the fins:* Holding the squid by the head, grasp the two soft fins and pull them up and away from the body (do not cut); they will pop right off.
2. *Remove the skin:* Grip the thin reddish skin between your thumb and index finger; lift and peel. This is a lot like peeling the label off a bottle. Or scrape the skin off with a dull knife.
3. *Remove the head:* Pull the head away from the body; it will separate naturally.
4. *Clean the body:* With a firm tug, pull the clear plastic-like cartilage out of the body. Rinse the body under cold running water to remove ink.
5. *Trim the tentacles:* Using a sharp knife cut off the tentacles as a whole cluster by slicing about ½ inch above where they are joined to the head, just below the eyes.

Now the bodies are ready to be cut into rings or stuffed. The tentacles can be left whole or halved lengthwise or chopped, depending on the recipe. If desired, skin and use the fins, too.

SQUID AND SPINACH PIZZA

Squid is plentiful and inexpensive, and this pizza is a good way to try it if you've never had it before. Here, squid rings and tentacles top a pizza along with fresh spinach, red peppers, and feta cheese. The spinach keeps its deep green color, the peppers stay bright red, and the squid and feta are creamy white, making this pizza as pretty as it is tasty.

Makes one 12-inch to 14-inch round pizza

Crust:

> *Olive oil, to wipe pan and brush over dough*
> *1 teaspoon cornmeal, for pizza pan*
> *1 batch Basic Pizza Dough (page 24) or*
> *one bag of dough from market*

Topping:

> *½ cup tomato sauce*
> *1 tablespoon anchovy paste*
> *2 cloves garlic, pressed*
> *4 cups, packed, washed, and*
> *torn fresh spinach*
> *½ cup loosely packed whole basil leaves*

> *¾ pound cleaned squid (see page 25)*
> *2 large red bell peppers, roasted,*
> *peeled, and seeded (see page 209)*
> *½ pound feta cheese*
> *¼ cup grated Parmesan cheese*
> *1 tablespoon olive oil*

✎ Preheat oven to 450 degrees.

✎ Prepare the pizza pan by wiping the surface with a little olive oil and sprinkling with cornmeal. Roll the dough out and fit it into the pan, crimping and shaping the edge to desired thickness. Brush the dough with 1 tablespoon of olive oil.

✎ In a small bowl mix the tomato sauce with the anchovy paste and garlic. Spread over the pizza dough, starting ½ inch in from the edge.

≫ Evenly distribute the spinach over the tomato sauce. Chop the basil coarsely and sprinkle over the spinach.

≫ Cut the cleaned squid bodies into rings, approximately ¼ inch wide. Cut the tentacles into ½-inch lengths. Distribute evenly over the spinach and basil.

≫ Cut the peppers into long narrow strips and then into ½-inch sections. Distribute evenly over the pizza. Crumble the feta cheese and sprinkle over the pizza; follow with the Parmesan cheese.

≫ Sprinkle the olive oil over the pizza, concentrating on the squid pieces.

≫ Bake for about 20 minutes, or until the crust is done, the squid is white, and the top of the pizza is steaming hot. Cut and serve immediately.

CLAM AND POTATO PIZZA

Potatoes on a pizza may sound odd, but when sliced paper thin, they become a tender bed beneath the rest of the more textured toppings—and a perfect backdrop to the flavors of the clams, bacon, and onions.

You can buy minced clams at your fish market to save time, but I think you'll be more pleased with the results if you buy littlenecks in the shell and cook them at home. You'll also end up with some broth to add to your fish stock collection. If you buy minced clams, three-quarters of a pound is enough for this pizza.

Makes one 12-inch to 14-inch round pizza

Crust:

> *Olive oil, for wiping pan and brushing dough*
> *1 teaspoon cornmeal, for pizza pan*
> *1 batch Basic Pizza Dough (page 24) or*
> *   1 bag of dough from the market*

Topping:

3 dozen littleneck clams in the shell,   *1 tablespoon finely chopped fresh*
     cleaned and steamed (see page 142)   *parsley*
4 slices lean bacon   *2 teaspoons finely chopped fresh*
¼ pound potatoes (2 medium potatoes)   *marjoram*
Salt and freshly ground black pepper   *3 tablespoons grated Parmesan cheese*
1 medium onion, cut into thin slivers   *1 tablespoon olive oil*
     (about ⅔ cup)

⊱ Preheat oven to 450 degrees.

⊱ Prepare the pizza pan by wiping the surface with olive oil and sprinkling with corn-meal. Roll the dough out and fit it into the pan, crimping and shaping the edge to the desired thickness. Brush the dough with 1 tablespoon of olive oil.

⊱ When the clams are cool enough to handle, remove the meat and set aside. If the clams are very small, leave them whole; otherwise chop them coarsely.

⊱ Cut the bacon into 1-inch chunks and cook in a skillet over medium heat until it has rendered fat but has not become crisp. Using a slotted spoon remove the bacon from the skillet and set aside.

⊱ Using a food processor or mandoline cut the potatoes into paper-thin slices. Arrange the slices in overlapping circles over the pizza dough, starting ½ inch from the outside edge. Sprinkle a small amount of salt and pepper over the potatoes. Next, evenly distribute the bacon over the potatoes, then the clams (drain the clams if you are using already-minced from the market), then the onion. Sprinkle the pizza with the herbs and Parmesan cheese, and drizzle the olive oil over all.

⊱ Bake for about 20 minutes, or until the crust is done, the potatoes are tender, the bacon is crisp, and the top of the pizza is steaming hot. Cut and serve immediately.

OYSTER AND ONION PIZZA

This pizza calls for few ingredients, but each has such a distinctive flavor that the combination is a good example of "less is more." The onion cooks down into a savory bed for the oysters, and both are complemented by two flavorful cheeses.

Makes one 12-inch to 14-inch round pizza

Crust:

> *Olive oil for wiping pan*
> *1 teaspoon cornmeal, for pizza pan*
> *1 batch Basic Pizza Dough (page 24) or*
> *1 bag of dough from the market*

Topping:

> *2 cloves garlic, pressed*
> *2 tablespoons olive oil*
> *3 tablespoons crumbled*
> *Gorgonzola cheese*
> *3 medium onions,*
> *sliced extremely thin*

> *¾ pound shucked raw oysters,*
> *drained, with liquid reserved,*
> *and coarsely chopped*
> *¼ cup grated Asiago cheese*
> *1 tablespoon finely chopped fresh parsley*
> *1 teaspoon finely chopped fresh thyme*

Preheat oven to 450 degrees.

Prepare the pizza pan by wiping the surface with olive oil and sprinkling with cornmeal. Roll the dough out and fit it into the pan, crimping and shaping the edge to desired thickness.

In a small bowl combine the garlic with 1 tablespoon of olive oil and spread over the pizza dough. Sprinkle the Gorgonzola evenly over the dough ½ inch in from the edge. Arrange the onions over the cheese in overlapping circles. Evenly distribute the drained oysters (save the liquid for fish stock) over the onions. Sprinkle with the Asiago cheese, parsley, and thyme. Drizzle the remaining tablespoon of olive oil over all.

Bake for about 20 minutes, or until the crust is done, the onions are tender, the oysters are cooked, and the top of the pizza is steaming hot. Cut and serve immediately.

SHRIMP AND EGGPLANT PIZZA

The exquisite combination of shrimp, roasted eggplant, fresh basil, and goat cheese make this pizza a standout. The eggplant can be prepared a few hours in advance to save time. *Makes one 12-inch to 14-inch pizza*

Crust:

Olive oil for wiping pan and brushing dough
1 teaspoon cornmeal, for pizza pan
1 batch Basic Pizza Dough (page 24) or
    1 bag of dough from the market

Topping:

1 large eggplant
    (about 1¼ to 1½ pounds)
5 tablespoons olive oil
¾ pound medium shrimp,
    shelled and deveined
1 clove garlic, pressed

½ cup tomato sauce
¼ cup grated Asiago cheese
½ cup goat cheese
2 tablespoons finely chopped fresh basil
1 tablespoon finely chopped
    fresh parsley

➢ Prepare the pizza pan by wiping the surface with olive oil and sprinkling with cornmeal. Roll the dough out and fit it into the pan, crimping and shaping the edge to desired thickness. Brush the dough with 1 tablespoon of olive oil.

➢ Prepare the eggplant: Cut the eggplant lengthwise into ¼- to ⅜-inch slices. Brush with 4 tablespoons of olive oil and place on a jelly roll pan. Cook under a broiler, turning once, until golden on both sides—3 to 5 minutes per side. Remove pan to a cooling rack.

➢ In a large bowl toss the shrimp with the garlic and remaining tablespoon of olive oil. Cover and set aside.

➢ Preheat oven to 450 degrees.

⨯⊃ Starting ½ inch in from the edge, spread the tomato sauce over the oiled pizza dough. Cut the broiled eggplant slices into 1-inch strips and then cut the strips into 1-inch pieces. Distribute evenly over the sauce, including any juices that form in the pan. Sprinkle half of the Asiago cheese over the eggplant. Next, evenly distribute the shrimp over the eggplant, and top with the rest of the Asiago cheese. Place little pieces of goat cheese over all and sprinkle with the herbs. Drizzle any garlic oil left from the shrimp marinade over all.

⨯⊃ Bake for about 20 minutes, or until the crust is done, the shrimp are cooked, and the top of the pizza is steaming hot. Cut and serve immediately.

Nets drying, Gloucester, Massachusetts, 1920s.

This used to be a common sight when nets were made of natural fibers. The nets had to be hung up to dry to prevent rotting. This was also a handy way to mend a net. Nowadays, nets are made of synthetic fibers that resist rotting, and the need for drying racks has virtually disappeared.

TUNA AND PESTO PIZZA

I developed this pizza recipe one summer when a friend brought by more fresh tuna than I could fit in the freezer. The tangy taste of pesto is a good partner for this rich fish, as is the liberal topping of robust vegetables—onion, plum tomatoes, and red bell pepper.
Makes one 12-inch to 14-inch pizza

Crust:

> *Olive oil for wiping pan and brushing dough*
> *1 teaspoon cornmeal, for pizza pan*
> *1 batch Basic Pizza Dough (page 24) or*
> *   1 bag of dough from the market*

Topping:

> *½ cup pesto (see Basic Pesto, page 206)*
> *¾ pound fresh tuna, cut into*
> *   1-inch by ¼-inch chunks*
> *1 red bell pepper, cut into ¼-inch by*
> *   1-inch strips (about ⅔ cup)*

> *¾ cup diced plum tomatoes*
> *1 medium onion, thinly sliced*
> *⅓ cup grated Asiago cheese*
> *⅓ cup grated mozzarella*

Preheat oven to 450 degrees.

Prepare the pizza pan by wiping the surface with olive oil and sprinkling with cornmeal. Roll the dough out and fit it into the pan, crimping and shaping the edge to desired thickness. Brush the dough with 1 tablespoon of olive oil.

Starting ½ inch in from the edge, spread the pesto over the dough. Evenly distribute the tuna over the pesto. Sprinkle the pepper strips over the pizza. Follow this with the diced plum tomatoes and onion. Sprinkle the grated cheeses evenly over all.

Bake for about 20 minutes, or until the crust is done, the tuna is cooked, and the top of the pizza is steaming hot. Cut and serve immediately.

3

Chowders, Bisques, Soups, and Stews

Baiting a trawl for winter banks fishing, 1930s.

"Men who go in for this life are not worrying overmuch about being lost. . . . They would hardly be trying to make a living at bank fishing; at least they would not try for long and surely never at all in winter."

— James B. Connolly, *The Book of Gloucester Fishermen*

In this chapter you'll find fish chowders and velvety bisques, elegant soups, and hearty stews. Seven different shellfish (mussels, clams, oysters, scallops, crab, squid, and shrimp) and five different finfish—with suggestions for even more substitutions—are used in the recipes. They range from the least expensive to the most expensive seafood and cover the four seasons as well. And all are suitable as the main course for dinner.

To make good soup from scratch you will need a large stockpot (stainless steel is best) or a Dutch oven (these are made of cast iron or of porcelain-coated cast iron and can be used on top of the stove or in the oven), a colander, a fine-mesh sieve, and cheesecloth.

You can buy commercially prepared fish stock, but I recommend that you make your own. You won't believe how easy it is, and you will end up with a much superior product. Fish stock is made by cooking fish racks (the body of the fish after it is filleted) and/or shellfish shells with a combination of vegetables, herbs, water, and wine. It forms the base for seafood soups and chowders, and can also be used as the base for making seafood sauces and for cooking risotto.

If you're not experienced at making soup from scratch, start with the Oven-Baked Fish Chowder (page 38); it's the easiest. Add some good bread and a salad, and you have a healthful dinner.

Making Fish Stock

There is something satisfying about making fish stock. Perhaps it is the way a handful of simple, homely items—fish bones, some root vegetables, and water—are transformed during the cooking process into a sophisticated broth of subtle flavors.

To make stock well, get in the habit of saving food by-products that you might normally throw away: the shells of peeled shrimp, fish racks (bones and skin), cooking liquid from steaming shellfish (in recipes where the cooking liquid is not used), and vegetable trimmings such as celery leaves and parsley stems. All of these can be stored in the freezer—in airtight packages, labeled and dated—until you are ready to make stock.

The vegetables and herbs used to create stock are generally discarded, along with the fish parts, after the stock is made. (*Sometimes* they are removed, pureed, and added back to the strained stock, but this is an exception.)

Stock can be kept in your freezer and added to if the initial amount is too small for any recipe. It is perfectly fine to combine stocks made from different fish or shellfish; if anything, you'll get an even better result.

If you don't know how to fillet fish and don't want to learn, you can probably get fresh fish carcasses from your local fish market (these are left over from the filleting process). If you visit your fish market regularly and habitually make this request, it won't be long before they are automatically offered to you.

When you get home, either freeze the fish carcasses or place them in your stockpot with some water, wine, herbs, and vegetables. Let them simmer while you prepare the seafood you just purchased. The finished stock can then be stored in the refrigerator or freezer until you need it.

Note: A longer simmer does not make for a richer stock! Too much time can make it too strong or bitter. Thirty minutes is just right.

BASIC FISH STOCK

As a general rule, use 1 quart of water and 1 cup of white wine for each pound and a half of fish parts. Increase or decrease as needed; for example, for 2 pounds of fish parts use 6 cups of water and 1½ cups of wine, etc.

You can use just about any fish to make a stock, but avoid oily fish, like mackerel and bluefish. Some cooks recommend using only white fish, such as sole, but I think you can be a lot more bold than that. I like to use tautog (also called blackfish), or sea trout (also called weakfish), or cod. Experiment, and don't be afraid to use more than one kind of fish in the stock.

You can vary this basic recipe in many ways depending on your taste and what you have on hand. For instance, you can use vermouth instead of wine (but use a bit less), you can use leeks instead of onion, you can use nearly any fresh herb you like as well as the parsley, and so on.

Makes about 1 quart

> 1½ pounds fish carcass (head, tails,
>   bones, and skin)
> 1 quart water
> 1 cup dry white wine
> 1 onion, peeled but left whole
> 2 whole cloves
>
> 1 carrot, split lengthwise
> 1 stalk celery, split lengthwise
> 1 bay leaf
> ¼ teaspoon black peppercorns
> 3 sprigs of fresh parsley

Rinse the fish parts under cold running water and place in a large stockpot. Add the water and wine. Stud the onion with the cloves and add it to the pot along with the rest of the ingredients. Place over high heat and bring to a boil, then simmer, uncovered, for 30 minutes.

Strain the stock by pouring it into a large bowl through a fine-mesh sieve lined with 2 layers of dampened cheesecloth. Discard all solids. Refrigerate or freeze the stock until ready to use.

When you are ready to use the stock in a recipe, season it to taste with salt and pepper; the other ingredients and further reducing the stock will affect the flavor.

OVEN-BAKED FISH CHOWDER

Unlike more traditional recipes for chowder, this does not call for homemade fish stock, rendered salt pork, and hours of straining, tending, and simmering. With this recipe a few staple pantry items are combined with the fish of your choice and transformed, during a leisurely hour in the oven, to an exquisite stew.

This is rich and wonderful even when made with 2% milk, not light cream. You could also use evaporated skim milk.

Serves 6

2 pounds cod, haddock, hake, or any firm white fish fillets	4 tablespoons butter
3 cups diced potatoes	1½ teaspoons chopped fresh dill
1½ cups diced celery	¼ teaspoon freshly ground black pepper
1½ cups diced onion	½ cup dry white wine
1 bay leaf	2 cups boiling water or fish stock
1 teaspoon salt	1 clove garlic, finely minced
4 whole cloves	1 cup milk or light cream
	2 teaspoons chopped fresh parsley

➣ Preheat oven to 375 degrees.

➣ Rub your fingertips along the fish to feel for bones and remove any with tweezers. Place the fish fillets, whole, in a 4-quart Dutch oven or other ovenproof casserole that can be transferred later to the top of the stove. The fish will flake into bite-size pieces as it cooks; do not cut it. Add the vegetables and all the remaining ingredients except the milk or cream and parsley. Cover the casserole and bake for 1 hour.

➣ Transfer the Dutch oven to the top of the stove and place over low heat. Slowly stir in the milk or cream. Let sit over low heat for 5 to 10 minutes. Add the fresh parsley and serve immediately.

➣ Remove the cloves if you see them when you ladle out the soup. Make sure your dinner companions know to watch for them if you don't find them all.

Variations:

Follow this recipe as given the first time you make it, but after that you may want to improvise. Here are some ideas:

1. Add 1 cup of fresh corn kernels when you add the milk or cream.
2. Cook 3 slices of bacon, drain, and crumble. Sprinkle some over each serving.
3. Substitute fresh tarragon for the dill.
4. Add ½ cup of diced carrots to the ingredients before placing in the oven.
5. Add 1 cup of drained and chopped stewed tomatoes when adding the milk or cream.

Stern-trawler towing the net.

Seagulls hover in anticipation of the easy meal about to come their way. The photo was taken from a passing dragger at sea in the 1980s.

CLAM CHOWDER

There is certainly no shortage of recipes for clam chowder floating around New England, but this one is my idea of the quintessential chowder: simple and chock-full of clams, tender potatoes, and a flavorful but plain milk broth. As with any chowder or soup, this is even better the next day.

Serves 6 to 8

4 dozen live littleneck clams
1 cup water
1½ cups dry white wine
8 tablespoons butter
1½ cups chopped onions

4 cups diced peeled potatoes
½ teaspoon chopped fresh thyme
6 cups milk
Salt and pepper to taste

Scrub the clams with a stiff brush under cold running water to remove any grit.

Place the water and ½ cup of wine in a large stockpot and bring to a boil. Depending on the size of the pot, cook the clams in batches of a dozen or more by placing them in the pot, covering, and cooking over high heat for about 5 minutes. Lift the cover to check, and as the clams open, remove them from the pot with tongs and set aside in a large bowl. Discard any clams that fail to open. Reserve the cooking liquid.

When you have cooked all the clams and they are cool enough to handle, remove the meat. Pick over the clams still in the shell to catch any liquid; discard the shells as you go and place the meat in a separate bowl. Add all the juice from the picked clams to the liquid in the stockpot. Set a fine-mesh sieve lined with 2 layers of dampened cheesecloth over a large bowl and strain the broth through it. You should have 4 to 5 cups of liquid. Cover and set aside.

In a Dutch oven or heavy soup pot, melt the butter over medium heat. Add the onions and cook until tender and translucent but not browned. Add the strained clam broth and the remaining cup of wine. Bring to a boil and cook for 5 minutes to intensify the flavors.

Add the potatoes to the pot and return to a boil. Lower the heat to a simmer, cover, and cook for 10 to 15 minutes, or until the potatoes are tender but not falling apart.

⤜ Add the thyme, clams, and milk and continue to cook over very low heat, stirring occasionally, until the chowder is heated through; do not allow the chowder to boil. Season to taste with salt and pepper, and serve hot.

SEAFOOD CHOWDER

This chowder starts with rendered salt pork, an old-fashioned technique that adds tremendous flavor. The seafood here is a combination of scallops, quahogs, and monkfish (or any other firm white fish such as cod or haddock). I find that milk makes a perfectly satisfactory chowder, but for a richer version use light cream.
Serves 8

24 live quahogs (clams)	*½ teaspoon chopped fresh thyme*
1 cup water	*½ teaspoon chopped fresh marjoram*
½ cup dry white wine	*½ pound shucked scallops*
¼ pound salt pork	*½ pound fish (monkfish, cod, haddock,*
3 cups chopped onions	*or other firm white fish), cut in*
1 cup chopped celery	*1-inch cubes*
2 cups fish stock	*4 cups milk or light cream*
3 cups diced potatoes	*1 tablespoon butter*
1 tablespoon chopped fresh parsley	*Salt and pepper to taste*
1 bay leaf	

⤜ Scrub the quahogs under cold running water to remove any grit. In a large stockpot bring the water and wine to a boil. Add the quahogs, cover, and cook for about 5 minutes, or until the shells open. As they open, remove the clams with tongs and transfer to a large bowl to cool. Discard any clams that do not open. When the clams are cool enough to handle, remove the meat from them. Pick over the clams to catch the juices and place the meat in a separate bowl. Cover and refrigerate.

≫ Add any juices that collected from the cooked clams to the cooking liquid in the stock-pot. Place over high heat and bring to a boil. Simmer, uncovered, for 5 minutes to reduce the stock. Place a fine-mesh sieve lined with 2 layers of dampened cheesecloth over a large bowl. Pour the stock through it. Reserve 1 cup to use later in the chowder (the remainder can be added to your stock collection).

≫ Cut the salt pork into small cubes and cook, stirring occasionally, in a Dutch oven or heavy soup pot over medium heat. When the salt pork is golden and crisp and has rendered its fat, add the onions and continue to cook until they are tender but not browned. Add the celery, stir, and cook for another minute. Pour in the reserved cup of cooking liquid from the quahogs and add the fish stock, potatoes, and herbs. Bring the mixture to a boil, lower the heat, cover, and simmer for about 10 minutes, or until the potatoes are tender but not mushy.

≫ At this point the chowder base can be refrigerated until you are ready to finish it. To finish the chowder, add the scallops and cubed fish. Bring the mixture to a simmer, cover, and cook over medium-low heat for about 3 minutes. Chop the cooked quahogs and add them to the chowder along with the milk and butter. Season to taste with salt and pepper. Stir while the mixture becomes thoroughly heated; do not allow it to boil. When hot, ladle into soup bowls and serve immediately.

Wooden Boats and Iron Men

During the last half of the nineteenth century, Gloucester, Massachusetts, was home to the largest fleet of fishing schooners and earned the title of the leading fishing port in the world, in terms of landings. The fleet fished Georges Bank and the Grand Banks, engaging in dory fishing and seining. The schooners, beautiful and sleek, were referred to as "able handsome ladies" in their day and built to be fast. Their catches were legendary, but so was the loss of life for those who went to sea on them; between 1830 and 1897 alone nearly seven hundred vessels were lost and close to four thousand men.

OYSTER CHOWDER

A steaming bowl of oyster chowder is the perfect antidote to a long day spent outside in the cold. This hearty chowder is surprisingly quick to assemble and is rich and satisfying. Add some bread, warm from the oven, and a crisp romaine lettuce salad, and you have a complete meal.

Serves 6

½ pound bacon, cooked, drained, and crumbled (with drippings reserved)
3 cups diced potatoes
½ cup diced carrot
1 cup chopped onion
½ cup chopped celery

½ teaspoon salt
½ teaspoon freshly ground black pepper
1 cup water
4 cups milk
1 pint shucked oysters, in liquid

Place 3 tablespoons of the bacon drippings in a large soup pot or Dutch oven. Add the potatoes, carrot, onion, and celery, and cook over medium heat. When the potatoes are tender, add the salt, pepper, and water. Bring to a boil, cover, and cook at a simmer for 15 minutes. Add the milk and stir until the mixture returns to a simmer. Add the oysters with their liquid and continue cooking for about 5 minutes, or until the edges of the oysters curl. Sprinkle in the crumbled bacon just before serving. Serve immediately in hot soup bowls.

CRAB BISQUE

This bisque gets its beautiful color and creamy texture from pureed butternut squash, an ingredient that makes a perfect flavor backdrop for the crab. As a whimsical touch, each serving of bisque is sprinkled with a few butternut squash "croutons"—small dice that at first glance appear to be toasted bread.

The crabs here will yield about 2 cups of picked meat; rock crabs are inexpensive and readily available all year round in New England.

Serves 4

6 cups water	*½ cup chopped celery*
4 live rock crabs (about 4 pounds)	*½ cup dry white wine*
1 bay leaf	*1 tablespoon cognac*
1 medium-large butternut squash	*1 cup milk or light cream*
3 tablespoons butter	*½ teaspoon nutmeg*
½ cup chopped onion	*Salt and pepper to taste*

✎ In a large stockpot over high heat, bring the water to a boil. Add the crabs and bay leaf, and cover. When the water returns to a boil, lower the heat to medium and cook for 12 minutes. Take the pot off the heat, remove the crabs from the pot, and transfer them to a bowl. Reserve the liquid, leaving it in the stockpot.

✎ Peel and chop the butternut squash into neat ½-inch cubes. (Some of the squash later becomes a garnish, so it is important for it to be diced neatly and evenly.) Cook until just tender, not mushy, using a steamer, microwave, or oven. Set aside ½ cup of squash to use later as "croutons"; transfer the remainder to a large bowl and set aside.

✎ Melt 2 tablespoons of the butter in a large (10-inch or 12-inch) skillet over medium heat. Add the onion and celery and cook over medium heat, stirring occasionally, until completely soft but not browned. Transfer the vegetables to the large bowl of squash. Do not wash the skillet; you will use it to cook the shells.

✎ When the crabs are cool enough to handle, pick out the meat and set it aside. Remove and discard the lungs and other nonedible parts. Break the shells into small pieces and set aside.

≫ Add the remaining tablespoon of butter to the skillet and melt it over medium heat. Place as many of the broken crab shells in the skillet as will comfortably fit, allowing room for stirring. Place the rest of the shells in the stockpot with the reserved cooking liquid. Cook the shells in the skillet over medium heat, stirring occasionally, for 20 minutes. Simultaneously, bring the reserved stock with the remainder of the shells to a simmer and cook over low heat, partially covered, for 10 minutes.

≫ Add 1 cup of stock (use a ladle to avoid the shells), wine, and cognac to the shells in the skillet and continue cooking over medium-low heat for 15 minutes. Remove from the heat and strain through a sieve lined with a double layer of dampened cheesecloth, directly into a soup pot. Strain the pot of stock with shells through a sieve lined with a double layer of dampened cheesecloth, reserving 2 cups of stock for the bisque.

Hauling in a fish trap, Point Judith Harbor, Rhode Island, 1935.

This method of fishing has changed little over the last 2,000 years.

↬ Place the cooked vegetables and ½ cup of the reserved stock in a food processor or blender and puree until completely smooth. Strain through a fine-mesh sieve and add this to the wine stock mixture in the soup pot. Add the remaining 1½ cups of reserved stock to the soup pot along with the crabmeat. Bring to a simmer and slowly add the milk. Season with nutmeg, salt, and pepper. When ready, ladle into hot soup bowls and top each serving with a few of the squash "croutons." Serve immediately.

SHRIMP AND SCALLOP BISQUE

Seared shrimp and scallops are the only solids in this creamy bisque. The base is thickened with pureed vegetables, and the tomatoes and splash of cream lend a beautiful pink color. The base can be made a day ahead.

This recipe is a modification of one by Tracey Seaman, from a 1994 issue of *Food & Wine.*

Serves 6 to 8

4 carrots	3 sprigs of fresh parsley
4 stalks celery	3 cups water
2 onions	2½ cups fish stock
4 cloves garlic	One 16-ounce can plum tomatoes
1 small fennel bulb (yield: about ½ cup)	1 teaspoon chopped fresh thyme
2 tablespoons butter	2 teaspoons chopped fresh parsley
1 pound medium shrimp, peeled and deveined, with shells reserved	½ cup light cream
	Salt and pepper to taste
3 cups dry white wine	2 tablespoons olive oil
2 sprigs of thyme	½ pound scallops

↬ Prepare the vegetables for the stock: Clean and chop 3 carrots, 3 stalks of celery, and 1 onion. Peel and mince the garlic. Trim and core the fennel bulb and chop coarsely.

 Heat the butter in a large soup pot over medium heat. Add the prepared vegetables and cook, stirring occasionally, for about 10 minutes, or until softened but not browned. Add the shrimp shells, wine, thyme and parsley sprigs. Bring the mixture to a boil and cook for 2 minutes. Add the water, bring to a boil, cover, lower the heat, and simmer for 20 minutes.

 Pour the stock through a fine-mesh strainer and discard the solids. Return the strained stock to the pot. Add the fish stock, tomatoes with their juices, and the remaining carrot, celery, and onion. Bring to a boil. Lower the heat, cover, and simmer for 30 minutes. Remove the pot from the heat and with a slotted spoon transfer the vegetables to a food processor. Puree thoroughly and then add the puree to the stock.

 Add the chopped thyme and parsley, and the cream; season to taste with salt and pepper. At this point you can refrigerate the soup for 24 hours or until you are ready to finish the soup.

 To finish, bring the soup to a gentle simmer over low heat. In a large skillet heat the olive oil over medium heat. When hot, add the scallops and cook, turning them with tongs, until they have a golden crust. Remove to a platter and add the shrimp to the skillet. Cook the shrimp until they are pink with golden edges. Remove from the heat.

 Ladle the hot soup into warmed soup bowls and place a few shrimp and scallops in each serving. Serve immediately.

Weather — a Fisherman's Constant Working Companion

Bad weather doesn't just keep fishermen ashore or make fishing trips more difficult, it can put a fisherman out of business. Gear that is generally left in the water and for which there is no insurance (lobster traps and gill nets, for instance) is worth tens of thousands of dollars and can be destroyed and lost by a bad storm or hurricane. Hurricanes can so dramatically change a fish population that, coming after other hardships, a fisherman can be wiped out by the effects.

MUSSEL SOUP

I keep a three-ring binder of recipes clipped from newspapers and magazines. This one, from a 1988 issue of *Gourmet,* sat untried for years until late one March when I broke one of my cardinal rules of *never* trying a new recipe for a party (a rule I am always forgetting). Luckily, the soup was wonderful.

The flavorful broth has a subtle lemon flavor and lots of fresh parsley, and its tastes are a delight after the gray days of winter. Put a vase of fresh daffodils on the table when you serve this, and you and your guests will know spring has arrived.

Serves 4 to 6

5 pounds live mussels, scrubbed and debearded
1 cup dry white wine
3 tablespoons butter
1 cup chopped onion

½ cup milk
½ cup chopped fresh flat-leaf parsley (do not use dry)
1½ tablespoons fresh lemon juice
Salt and pepper to taste

≫ Following the directions on page 142, cook the mussels in the wine. Pick the mussels from the shells. While doing this, check for any grit or beard that you may have missed. Set the mussels aside. Add any juices caught while picking the meat to the cooking liquid in the pot. Pour this through a fine-mesh sieve lined with a double layer of dampened cheesecloth into a 2-quart measuring cup. Add enough cold water to measure 4 cups in all. Set aside.

≫ Melt the butter in a large soup pot over medium heat. When it sizzles, add the onion and cook until tender and translucent, not browned. Add the mussel stock and bring to a boil. Lower the heat and simmer, covered, for 20 minutes.

≫ Slowly pour the milk into the soup pot, whisking constantly. Add the parsley, lemon juice, mussels, and salt and pepper to taste. Continue to cook over low heat for 5 minutes, or until the soup is thoroughly heated. Do not boil! Serve immediately.

LINGUICA, LITTLENECK CLAM, AND MUSSEL SOUP

This soup is full of the rich, warm flavor of linguica, a spicy Portuguese sausage. Littleneck clams and mussels are added to the soup pot and cooked, in the shell, after all the other ingredients have been incorporated, making this dish as handsome as it is flavorful. Be sure to have crusty bread on the table to dunk in the soup.

If you prefer, use all clams instead of mussels and clams.

Serves 4

1 tablespoon butter	*½ teaspoon chopped fresh marjoram*
1 tablespoon oil	*1 tablespoon chopped fresh parsley*
1½ cups diced potatoes	*1 teaspoon paprika*
Salt and pepper	*1 tablespoon Worcestershire sauce*
½ cup chopped onion	*½ cup red wine*
¼ pound linguica, split lengthwise	*3 cups fish stock*
* and cut in 1-inch pieces*	*16 live littleneck clams, scrubbed clean*
2 cloves garlic, pressed	*20 live mussels (with shells about*
1 red bell pepper, chopped	* 2–2½ inches), scrubbed and debearded*
½ teaspoon chopped fresh thyme	

In a Dutch oven or heavy soup pot heat the butter and oil over medium heat. Add the potatoes, sprinkle with a little salt and pepper, and cook, stirring occasionally, until lightly browned (about 3 minutes). Add the onion and continue cooking, stirring occasionally, until the onion is tender and translucent. Add the linguica, garlic, and red pepper, and cook until the linguica starts to curl and the pepper is tender. Add the herbs, Worcestershire sauce, and red wine. Continue cooking over medium heat, stirring occasionally, until the liquid is reduced by nearly half. Add the fish stock and bring the mixture to a boil. Add the clams, cover, lower the heat, and cook for 7 minutes. Add the mussels, cover, and cook for an additional 3 minutes, or until they open. (Discard any clams and mussels that do not open.) Serve immediately.

To serve:

✎ Use tongs to place a few clams and mussels in each soup bowl (the shells will be open but still hinged together, with the meat clinging to one of the shells). Stir the soup and ladle it into the soup bowls.

SEAFOOD GAZPACHO

Gazpacho is a chilled soup, chock-full of summer vegetables and herbs. Here, the gazpacho base is made in advance and chilled, allowing the flavors to develop. The seafood is coated with an orangy marinade, then pan-seared (or grilled, if you prefer). You can use any combination of seafood to equal 1½ pounds. When cooled, it is added to the soup as it is served. You can do most of the steps for this soup in advance—always a plus, especially during the heat of summer.

Serves 6

For the gazpacho base:

4 cups tomato juice
1 cup chopped red onion
2 cups diced tomatoes, large
  beefsteak type
1 cup chopped green bell pepper
1 cup diced cucumber
1 large clove garlic, pressed

2 tablespoons olive oil
1 tablespoon fresh lemon juice
1 tablespoon fresh lime juice
2 tablespoons red wine vinegar
¼ cup finely chopped fresh parsley
1 tablespoon finely chopped fresh basil
Salt and pepper to taste

For the marinade:

1 cup orange juice
2 teaspoons grated orange zest
2 teaspoons honey

4 tablespoons olive oil
1 clove garlic, pressed
1 teaspoon finely chopped fresh marjoram

Seafood:

1 pound monkfish, cut in 1-inch cubes
½ pound medium shrimp, peeled
  and deveined or
½ pound shucked scallops or
½ pound squid rings and tentacles

To sauté the seafood:

1 or 2 tablespoons olive oil

To make the gazpacho:

❧ Combine the tomato juice, vegetables, 2 tablespoons of olive oil, lemon and lime juices, vinegar, and seasonings in a large bowl. Transfer in batches to a food processor fitted with the metal blade and process by pulsing until the mixture is smoother than when first combined but still contains some chunks. Return to a large bowl, cover, and chill for at least 2 hours or overnight.

To marinate the seafood:

❧ Combine all the marinade ingredients in a bowl and whisk until well blended. Arrange the seafood in a single layer in a nonreactive pan. Pour the marinade over the fish, cover, and refrigerate for at least 1 hour or overnight, occasionally basting the seafood with the marinade.

To cook the seafood:

❧ Heat 1 tablespoon of olive oil in a large, heavy skillet over medium heat. When hot, add the seafood in batches and sear, turning it with tongs, until it is thoroughly cooked and has a nice golden crust. The monkfish will be firm, white inside and golden outside; the shrimp will be pink with some golden edges; the scallops will be white with a golden crust; and the squid will be opaque white with some golden edges. The squid will cook the fastest, in about 2 minutes; the other seafood will take longer, about 3 to 5 minutes. If needed, add the remaining tablespoon of oil while cooking. As the seafood is cooked, transfer to a platter to cool thoroughly before serving.

To serve:

✎ Place a portion of seafood in each soup plate. Ladle chilled gazpacho over it and serve immediately.

Iced up—winter fishing trip, 1990s.

Winter fishing presents a whole new set of challenges and hazards for New England fishermen. Ice forms on the deck and in the rigging, making the deck slippery and freezing deck hatches in place; ice in the rigging is a particular danger because it can make a boat top heavy, and falling hunks of ice can injure the men working on deck. Here, a fisherman uses a stream of seawater to clear ice from a passageway.

NEW ENGLAND FISH AND SHELLFISH STEW

The beauty of this stew is a broth so flavorful you'd be happy to eat it on its own, but each serving is literally overflowing with seafood—chunks of fish, littleneck clams in the shell, squid, and shrimp—making it quite beautiful to behold. You can prepare the base ahead of time, and when you are ready to finish the dish, add the fish; it cooks fairly quickly.

I think this combination of seafood makes a perfect blend, but substitute as you wish: The clams can be mussels, scallops can be substituted for some of the shrimp and/or squid, and you can use any firm-fleshed fish of your choice for the fish chunks, including swordfish. Delicate fillets, such as flounder, are not suitable because they break into pieces when cooked in the broth.

Serves 6

3 pounds whole fish—any one or a
   combination of tautog, sea trout,
   sea bass, haddock, cod, and the like
½ cup olive oil
½ cup thinly sliced onion
2 cloves garlic, pressed
½ pound medium shrimp
½ cup dry white wine
½ cup water

½ cup white wine vinegar
2 cups chopped stewed tomatoes
   with their liquid
12 littleneck clams, scrubbed clean
1 pound cleaned squid, cut in
   ½-inch rings, tentacles separated
2 tablespoons chopped fresh parsley
Salt and pepper to taste

⮞ Clean and fillet the whole fish, reserving the carcass as well as the fillets. Set both aside.

⮞ In a Dutch oven or heavy soup pot heat the olive oil over medium heat. Add the onion and garlic, and cook until the onion is tender and translucent, and the garlic is fragrant but not browned. With a slotted spoon remove the vegetables and transfer to a bowl. Set aside.

⮞ Peel and devein the shrimp. Place the fish parts (carcass, head, tail, and skin) and shrimp shells in the same pot the onion and garlic were cooked in and cook over medium-high heat, stirring occasionally, for about 5 minutes. Add half of the wine (¼ cup) and continue cooking until slightly reduced. Add the water, stir, and cook for another 2 minutes.

Remove from the heat and pour into a fine-mesh sieve set over a large bowl, pressing on the solids with a wooden spoon. Discard the solids and strain the mixture one more time through a fine-mesh sieve lined with a double layer of dampened cheesecloth. Set aside. Do not wash the pot used to cook the fish parts.

⊱ Return the onion/garlic mixture to the pot. Add the remaining ¼ cup of wine and the vinegar, stir, and cook over medium heat until the liquid is reduced by nearly half. Add the strained stock, the tomatoes and their juice and bring to a simmer, cover, and cook over low heat for 5 minutes.

⊱ At this point the soup may be stored in the refrigerator until you are ready to finish it. Or you can proceed with the recipe if you are planning to serve it immediately.

⊱ Set the soup at a very low simmer. Cut the fish fillets into 2-inch pieces. Add them to the soup without stirring. Cover the pot and cook for 2 minutes. Remove the lid and add the shrimp and clams, again without stirring. Cover and cook an additional 10 minutes. Remove the lid, add the squid, cover, and simmer for 2 minutes. Add the parsley and season to taste with salt and pepper.

To serve:

⊱ Use tongs or a slotted spoon to place a couple of clams, shrimp, and pieces of fish in each soup plate before ladling in the rest of the stew. Serve immediately with crusty bread.

New England's Wealth from the Sea

New England's coastline may comprise only 7.3 percent of the total United States coast, but more than one-third of America's supply of finfish and shellfish comes from this uniquely productive territory. Among all professional American fishermen, 35 percent are employed in the North Atlantic fisheries.

MONKFISH WINTER STEW

Not that many years ago monkfish was unknown to most Americans although popular in other countries. Fortunately, that has changed.

This soup would be good any time of the year, but the warm flavor of cayenne pepper makes it especially good during cold weather.

I first made this with monkfish but have since found tautog, cod, and even bluefish to be wonderful substitutions. When you choose a fish other than monkfish, be sure it is firm enough not to come apart into little shreds while cooking.
Serves 4

1 tablespoon olive oil
2 tablespoons butter
1⅓ cups chopped onions
1 cup chopped celery
1 clove garlic, pressed
3 cups washed, sorted, and torn
*   fresh spinach*
1-pound can crushed tomatoes with
*   their juice*

3½ cups fish stock
1 bay leaf
1 teaspoon chopped fresh thyme
¼ teaspoon cayenne pepper
1 pound monkfish, cut in 1-inch cubes
¼ cup chopped fresh parsley
1 tablespoon chopped fresh tarragon
1 cup uncooked tubettini pasta
Salt and pepper to taste

In a Dutch oven or heavy soup pot heat the oil and butter over medium heat. Add the onions, celery, and garlic, and cook, stirring occasionally, until the vegetables are tender and fragrant but not browned. Add the spinach and cook until wilted. Add the tomatoes, fish stock, bay leaf, thyme, and cayenne pepper, stir, and bring the mixture to a boil. When it reaches a boil, lower the heat, cover the pot, and simmer for 10 minutes. Add the fish chunks, parsley, tarragon, and pasta. Cover and continue to cook over medium-low heat for about 5 minutes, or until the fish and pasta are done. Season to taste with salt and pepper. Serve immediately.

4

Salads

Fishermen enjoying a pickup race with the Coast Guard off Point Judith, Rhode Island, in 1936.

Fishermen don't choose fishing simply as a way to make a living. They choose it because they love being on the water and "messing about in boats" as much as any yachtsman.

Classic Lobster Salad

Shrimp and Avocado Salad

Grilled Tuna Salad

Poached Salmon Salad

Squid Salad

Layered Seafood Salad

Mussel and Potato Salad

Scallop, Green Bean, and Potato Salad with Warm Thyme Dressing

Warm Balsamic Shrimp Salad

Oyster Spinach Salad

Seared Scallops and Baby Greens Salad

Shrimp, Corn, and Black Bean Salad

Skate and French Lentil Salad

Scallops

Skate, Often Overlooked

The salads in this chapter are main-course dishes and, in some cases, can also be used to make sandwiches. Making a meal of a robust salad and good bread is becoming acceptable because in addition to being fairly quick to assemble, a salad dinner is a healthy way to eat. In many instances an equal or greater portion of vegetables than meat or seafood makes the salads high in fiber and vitamins, and relatively low in fat.

For family I don't hesitate to serve a seafood salad as a main course for lunch *or* dinner. But many of these recipes are perfectly appropriate as the entree for a casual dinner party or a Sunday afternoon luncheon.

The recipes here range from old standbys like Classic Lobster Salad (page 60) to newer dishes such as Shrimp, Corn, and Black Bean Salad (page 74). There are chilled salads, warm salads, salads served on crisp greens, and salads where the heat of the seafood (and/or the dressing) wilts the greens.

Once you try some of these combinations I think you'll start coming up with your own. Seafood salads can also be a wonderful way to use up leftover fish or to affordably serve the more expensive seafoods, and a good way to include lots of vegetables at a meal.

CLASSIC LOBSTER SALAD

There is nothing *nouveau* about this recipe, but in my opinion it's hard to improve on a classic. This is the way I learned to make lobster salad from my parents, with lobster left over from a steamed lobster dinner the night before. It works beautifully as a salad or as the filling for a grilled lobster roll.

It's so easy to cook an extra lobster or two when you're having steamed lobsters for dinner. Try it next time, and you can enjoy homemade lobster salad the next day.

Serves 4

1 pound cooked lobster meat, coarsely
  chopped (about 2 cups)
¼ cup minced yellow or red onion
½ cup finely diced celery
2 tablespoons finely chopped
  fresh parsley
½ cup mayonnaise

1 tablespoon fresh lemon juice
Salt and pepper to taste
1 head Boston lettuce or other
  tender-leaf lettuce
2 large tomatoes, cut into wedges
1 European cucumber, sliced

In a large bowl combine the lobster meat with the onion, celery, and parsley. Toss. Add the mayonnaise, lemon juice, and salt and pepper to taste, and toss to combine. Cover and refrigerate until ready to use.

To serve, place a few leaves of Boston lettuce on each plate. Spoon a mound of lobster salad into the middle of the lettuce. Surround the lobster salad with tomato wedges and cucumber slices. Serve.

SHRIMP AND AVOCADO SALAD

This dish makes a beautiful presentation for a special luncheon. Half of an avocado is piled to overflowing with shrimp salad, and the other half is fanned out decoratively beside it. If you do not know how to pick out a ripe avocado, ask your greengrocer for help.

I developed this salad as a way to use Maine shrimp, but they are not always available. If you can get them, great; otherwise, use the smallest Gulf shrimp. If the smallest shrimp you can get is "medium," cut them into thirds.

Serves 4

1 pound cleaned and cooked shrimp (see page 142), cooled	4 teaspoons fresh lemon juice
½ cup finely diced carrot	2 teaspoons finely chopped fresh parsley
½ cup julienned celery root (celeriac)	Salt and pepper to taste
¼ cup mayonnaise	4 perfectly ripe avocados
	1 lemon, cut into 8 wedges

In a large bowl toss the shrimp with the carrot and celery root. In a separate bowl whisk together the mayonnaise, lemon juice, parsley, and salt and pepper to taste. Pour the dressing over the shrimp mixture and toss gently to coat evenly. Cover and refrigerate until ready to use.

To serve:

Halve the avocados, and remove and discard the pit. Place half of an avocado on each plate; skin the other half, slice it into ¼-inch sections, and fan out on the plate next to the avocado still in its skin. Divide the shrimp salad into 4 portions and spoon into the avocado halves. The salad will be more than the avocado can hold, so let it fall onto the plate next to the fanned slices. Put 2 lemon wedges on each plate and serve.

GRILLED TUNA SALAD

If you're fond of tuna salad but have only made it with canned tuna, you're in for a treat. We always grill a little extra tuna just so we can make this the next day. You can substitute grilled swordfish for a variation.

If you don't have a grill, cook the tuna steaks in a grill pan.

Serves 4

1½ pounds tuna steaks, grilled and
    cooled (see page 104)

½ cup minced celery

¼ cup minced onion

1 tablespoon fresh lemon juice

½ cup mayonnaise

¼ cup chopped cornichons
    (small French pickles)

1 tablespoon chopped fresh parsley

1 teaspoon Worcestershire sauce

Salt and pepper to taste

In a large bowl flake the tuna. Add the celery and onion, and toss gently. In a separate bowl mix the lemon juice, mayonnaise, cornichons, parsley, Worcestershire sauce, and salt and pepper to taste. Add this to the tuna mixture and toss gently to coat.

Use for sandwiches or as a salad on a bed of lettuce.

POACHED SALMON SALAD

Cold poached salmon is one of life's simple pleasures. Here it makes a tasty salad with tender peas, spring potatoes, and lots of fresh dill — perfect for a spring lunch, or light dinner. The salmon can be poached a day ahead.

Serves 4

1 pound salmon fillet

Poaching liquid:

6 cups water	*¼ teaspoon peppercorns*
1 cup dry white wine	*1 teaspoon salt*
1 onion, quartered	*1 bay leaf*
1 carrot, sliced in 4 sections	*¼ cup fresh parsley*

Salad ingredients:

1 pound small red-skinned potatoes	*2 tablespoons chopped fresh dill*
1 box frozen peas, thawed but not cooked	*½ cup mayonnaise*
	1 tablespoon fresh lemon juice
½ cup chopped scallions	*Salt and pepper to taste*
¼ cup grated carrot	*1 head Bibb lettuce*
1 tablespoon chopped fresh parsley	*1 lemon, cut in wedges*

To poach the salmon:

➣ In a fish poaching pan with a rack or in a roasting pan, combine the water, wine, onion, carrot, and seasonings. Place over high heat and bring to a boil. Lower heat and simmer for 20 minutes. Allow to cool before poaching the salmon.

➣ Place the salmon on the rack in the poaching pan, or if you are using a roasting pan, place the salmon on a piece of heavy-duty foil to act as a rack before setting it in the poaching liquid. If the fish is not covered with liquid when it is set in the pan, add water until it is. Cover the pan and place over medium heat. Slowly bring to a boil (this should take about 15 minutes) and simmer for 1 minute. Turn off the heat and allow salmon to sit in the poaching liquid until it is cool enough to handle. Lift salmon out of poaching liquid and transfer to a platter; do not worry if the salmon breaks apart. Cover and refrigerate.

To make the salad:

➣ Place the whole potatoes in a steamer over boiling water and cook until tender, about 10 to 15 minutes. When cool enough to handle, peel and dice the potatoes. Transfer to a bowl and set aside to cool.

➣ When the salmon and potatoes have cooled thoroughly, assemble the salad.

✣ Remove and discard the skin from the poached salmon and flake the meat, removing any bones; set aside.

✣ In a large bowl combine the potatoes, peas, scallions, carrot, parsley, and dill. Add the mayonnaise and lemon juice, and toss to coat thoroughly. Add salt and pepper to taste.

✣ Arrange a bed of lettuce leaves on each plate. Top with a spoonful of the potato/pea mixture. Place a portion of flaked salmon meat over each and serve with lemon wedges.

The Sounding Lead

In the days before the advent of electronic chromatoscopes, lorans, and depth finders that fishermen now use to figure out exactly where they are, what's on the bottom, and what kind of fish are in the water, they relied on some rather ingenious devices to find rich fishing grounds. One of these was the sounding lead. It was a narrow cylindrical item, about 8 inches long and an inch in diameter, and made of lead. It was hollowed out at one end and had a line attached at the other, knotted at various intervals to determine depth. The hollow was filled with tallow, and when the lead was dropped overboard, it would dive nose first into the bottom. Whatever was on the bottom would become embedded in the tallow, and when the captain examined it—and more important, it is said, *smelled* it—he could tell the nature of the fishing grounds below them and whether to stay and fish, or move on.

Years ago, an old story goes, a couple of young crewmen on a Gloucester schooner thought they would trick their captain, so before leaving port they secretly filled the tallow with some soil from town. When the time came to present the captain with the sounding lead, the two young crewmen held their breath and prepared for a good laugh as the captain examined it. He closed his eyes and took a long whiff. Then, looking at them with great seriousness, he said, "According to this, I reckon we're directly over Mrs. Murphy's garden."

SQUID SALAD

Squid has a delicate flavor that can be lost in deep frying and overpowered in tomato sauce dishes. Here, sautéed squid is presented barely adorned. Tossed with a few fresh vegetables and a tangy balsamic vinaigrette, the squid takes center stage.
Serves 4 to 6

1½ cups cleaned and trimmed fresh
   broccoli rabe
1 tablespoon olive oil
1½ to 2 pounds cleaned squid, cut in
   ¼-inch rings, tentacles separated
   and cut in half (see page 25)
1 clove garlic, finely minced
1 tablespoon fresh lemon juice

Freshly ground black pepper
½ cup thinly sliced red onion
½ cup julienned roasted red bell pepper
   (1 large pepper) (see page 209)
⅓ cup pitted and halved black olives
¼ cup loosely packed and chopped
   flat-leaf parsley

Vinaigrette:

3 sun-dried tomatoes
1½ tablespoons balsamic vinegar
1½ tablespoons red wine vinegar
1 clove garlic, pressed
½ teaspoon salt

⅓ cup olive oil
1 tablespoon chopped fresh basil
3 cups mixed greens, including some
   arugula, if available

✻ Bring a large pot of lightly salted water to a boil. Add the broccoli rabe and cook at a boil for 3 minutes. Drain in a colander and plunge into a large pan of cold water to stop the cooking; set aside to drain.

✻ In a large, heavy skillet heat the oil over medium heat. When hot, add the squid rings and tentacles, and cook until the squid is opaque white with some golden edges. Transfer the squid to a plate to cool.

⅏ Chop the broccoli rabe into 1-inch pieces. Add it, with the garlic, to the same skillet used for the squid and cook over medium heat for about 2 minutes, turning occasionally with a spatula. Remove from the heat and add the lemon juice and some freshly ground black pepper; set aside to cool.

⅏ In a large bowl combine the cooled squid and broccoli rabe with the onion, pepper, olives, and parsley. Toss.

To make the vinaigrette:

⅏ Place the tomatoes in a glass bowl and add boiling water to just cover. Let sit 15 minutes. Drain off the liquid and chop the tomatoes very fine.

⅏ In a small bowl whisk together the rest of the ingredients. Add the tomatoes and stir. Pour over the squid salad and toss.

⅏ To serve, place some of the mixed greens on each plate. Toss the salad again before spooning a portion on each plate of greens. Serve with bread and wedges of ripe tomato.

Note: You may serve the salad while the ingredients are still slightly warm, or cover the salad and refrigerate for a while to allow the flavors to develop. Bring to room temperature before serving.

LAYERED SEAFOOD SALAD

This salad is an adaptation of a recipe from my Aunt Mitt called "the untossed salad." The original has always been a favorite in our house, and it seemed a natural candidate for a layer of seafood in place of the usual layer of hard-boiled eggs. The seafood layer can be any number of choices. When I make this with squid, I use more than when making it with scallops or other seafood.

The salad should be assembled in a glass bowl so that the colors and distinct layers show before serving. I use a straight-sided glass salad bowl, 10 inches across by 4½ inches high, but you could also use a trifle bowl.

This must be made a day before serving; put it together on a Saturday afternoon to enjoy the next day at a leisurely Sunday lunch.

Skip the sauté step if you are using lobster or crab.

Serves 4 to 6

1 tablespoon olive oil	¼ pound bacon, cooked and crumbled
1 tablespoon butter	1 large head red and green leaf lettuce,
1½ pounds squid rings, sautéed, or	washed and torn
1 pound shucked scallops, seared, or	1 box frozen peas, thawed but not
1 pound cooked lobster meat, coarsely	cooked
chopped, or	1 large red onion, cut into thin rings
1 pound cooked lump crabmeat or	½ cup mayonnaise
1 pound medium shrimp, peeled,	2 hard-boiled eggs, finely chopped
deveined, and sautéed	2 tablespoons capers
¼ cup dry white wine	¼ cup grated cheddar cheese
One 10-ounce bag fresh spinach,	¼ cup grated Asiago cheese
sorted and washed	Paprika to taste
2 teaspoons sugar	1 tablespoon finely chopped fresh
½ teaspoon salt	parsley

⊱ Heat the olive oil and butter in a large, heavy skillet over medium heat and add the squid (or scallops or shrimp). As soon as the seafood has developed a golden color, add the wine to the pan. Continue cooking until the wine has evaporated. Set aside.

⊱ Tear the spinach leaves in pieces and place in an even layer in a large, straight-sided glass salad bowl or trifle bowl. Sprinkle with 1 teaspoon of sugar and ¼ teaspoon of salt. Evenly distribute the crumbled bacon over the spinach, and over that layer the seafood. Next add a layer of the washed and torn lettuce, and sprinkle the remaining teaspoon of sugar and ¼ teaspoon of salt over that. Distribute the peas over the lettuce, and top them with a layer of onion rings. In a small bowl combine the mayonnaise with the chopped egg and capers, and carefully spread the mixture over the onion rings. Sprinkle with the grated cheeses. Top with a light sprinkle of paprika and the chopped parsley. Cover tightly with plastic wrap and refrigerate for at least 6 hours or overnight.

⊱ Cut into wedges to serve, making sure you get some of each layer.

MUSSEL AND POTATO SALAD

Potato salads are one of the great traditions of American summers. Here, steamed mussels are added, and the whole is blended with a tangy dressing. On a bed of greens and surrounded with fresh summer vegetables, this makes a tasty meal or a great addition to a picnic spread.

Serves 6 to 8

5 pounds live mussels, scrubbed, debearded, and cooked (see page 142), with ½ cup of cooking liquid reserved

7 tablespoons olive oil

3 pounds small red-skinned potatoes, steamed until tender

2 scallions, chopped

1 cup chopped celery

1 tablespoon minced shallot

1 clove garlic, minced

1 tablespoon chopped fresh flat-leaf parsley

2 tablespoons white wine vinegar

1 tablespoon fresh lemon juice

1 tablespoon Dijon mustard

1 teaspoon anchovy paste

3 tablespoons light cream

✒ Pick out the mussel meat, checking again for any grit or beards that you may have missed, and set aside.

✒ Combine the reserved ½ cup of mussel broth with 3 tablespoons of oil. Pour over the mussels, toss gently, and set aside.

✒ Dice the potatoes and place them in a large bowl. Add the mussels, scallions, and celery. Toss gently.

✒ In a separate bowl combine the shallot, garlic, parsley, remaining 4 tablespoons of olive oil, vinegar, lemon juice, mustard, anchovy paste, and cream. Blend well.

✒ Pour the dressing over the potato/mussel mixture and toss gently to coat evenly. Cover and refrigerate for at least 1 hour to allow the flavors to develop.

✒ Allow to sit at room temperature for 10 to 15 minutes before serving. Serve on a bed of lettuce, with wedges of tomato and cucumber.

Scallops

Whether you buy scallops shucked or in the shell, always remove the little crescent-shaped piece of gristle that adheres to the scallop meat itself. At first it will be hard to notice, but once you find it, it's easy to spot. This is perfectly edible but becomes rubbery when cooked. I set them aside as a treat for my dog.

SCALLOP, GREEN BEAN, AND POTATO SALAD WITH WARM THYME DRESSING

A warm thyme-flavored dressing is a delicious complement to this salad. The hearty flavors are perfect for a fall day, the time of year when bay scallops are harvested.
Serves 4 to 6

3 tablespoons butter
1 pound shucked scallops
¼ cup minced shallots
1¼ cups dry white wine
1¼ cups light cream
2 tablespoons finely chopped
   fresh thyme
Salt and pepper to taste
1 tablespoon olive oil

3 cups peeled and diced potatoes, boiled
   until just tender
1 pound green beans, blanched and cut
   into 1-inch pieces
1½ cups diced tomatoes (about 2 large
   beefsteak tomatoes)
1 head butter or Boston lettuce, washed
   and dried

✒ Heat 2 tablespoons of butter in a large, lightly oiled skillet. Add the scallops and cook in a single layer over medium heat, turning with tongs, until golden on all sides. Transfer to an ovenproof dish, cover loosely with foil, and place in a warm oven.

✒ Add the remaining tablespoon of butter to the skillet. Add the shallots and cook over medium heat until they are tender but not browned. Add the wine, raise the heat and bring to a boil, scraping the bottom of the pan with a wooden spoon to loosen any bits of scallop or shallot adhering to the bottom. Lower the heat and add the cream and thyme. Bring the mixture to a low simmer and continue to cook gently, stirring, until reduced by about one-third. Add salt and pepper to taste. Remove from heat and cover.

✒ Heat the olive oil in a large skillet. Add the potatoes and toss until evenly coated. Continue cooking the potatoes over medium heat until they start to take on a pale golden color. Add the green beans and continue cooking, turning with a spatula, until the potatoes are a deep golden color with a slight crispness to the edges and the green beans are hot. Remove from the heat and transfer immediately to a large bowl. Add the scallops, with any juices that have formed in the dish, and toss gently with a large spoon. Pour the thyme sauce over the mixture. Toss gently again, coating evenly. Add the diced tomatoes and toss until evenly distributed.

✒ Arrange the lettuce on individual plates. Top each with a portion of the warm scallop salad. Serve immediately.

WARM BALSAMIC SHRIMP SALAD

In this "wilted" salad, grilled shrimp top a bed of greens mixed with sliced avocado and tomato, and the whole is married with a warm dressing of balsamic vinegar and caramelized red onion slices.

A pound of jumbo shrimp is usually ten to twelve shrimp. You'll want to serve five shrimp per person, so when you go to your fish market, buy the shrimp by count, not weight.

Serves 2

3 cups mesclun or a mix of your
   favorite salad greens
1½ tablespoons fresh lemon juice
3 tablespoons balsamic vinegar
1 tablespoon plus 1 teaspoon sugar
6 tablespoons olive oil
½ large red onion, thinly sliced
1 clove garlic, coarsely chopped
10 jumbo shrimp, peeled and deveined
   (save peels for stock)

1 tablespoon finely chopped fresh
   basil leaves
2 tablespoons grated Parmesan
   cheese
Freshly ground black pepper to taste
½ cup Garlic Croutons (page 208)
1 ripe avocado, peeled and sliced
1 large ripe tomato or 2 small ones,
   washed and quartered

Arrange the cleaned greens on 2 large dinner plates and cover with a barely damp paper towel.

Combine the lemon juice, vinegar, and sugar in a glass measuring cup; stir and set aside.

Heat 3 tablespoons of olive oil in a skillet over medium heat. Add the onion slices and cook until soft but not browned. Remove onions with a slotted spoon and set aside. Add the garlic and shrimp to the hot skillet and sauté until the shrimp are pink and have golden edges, approximately 2 to 3 minutes. Remove the shrimp, place on a platter, and cover loosely with a foil tent. Let rest while you complete the dish (about 5 minutes).

Scoop the cooked garlic out of the pan and discard. Add the remaining 3 tablespoons of oil and heat until warm. Return the onion slices to the pan and turn off the heat. Pour in the vinegar mixture and stir.

Now assemble the salad: Remove the paper towel from the greens. Sprinkle the basil, Parmesan cheese, pepper, and croutons over the lettuce. Arrange the sliced avocado and tomato wedges around the edges of the plates. Place the warm shrimp over the salad, including any juices that have formed on the platter, and top with the warm dressing and onions from the pan. Serve immediately.

OYSTER SPINACH SALAD

This is a beautiful salad for fall. Oysters are at their peak, as are spinach, apples, and walnuts, and the flavors are perfect complements for one another. The vivid colors—deep green spinach and golden yellow cornmeal-crusted oysters—make a stunning presentation. This is one of those salads where the warm dressing "wilts" the greens. Serve with warm bread and a chardonnay or fumé wine.

Serves 4

1 pound shucked oysters
½ cup yellow cornmeal
One 10-ounce bag fresh spinach
6 slices lean bacon
*1 large red onion, halved and
    thinly sliced*
1 cooking apple, peeled and grated
1 tablespoon sugar
¼ cup cider vinegar

¼ cup dry white wine
¼ teaspoon dry mustard
Salt and pepper to taste
2 tablespoons butter
½ cup grated Asiago cheese
½ cup coarsely chopped walnuts, toasted
*1 tablespoon finely chopped fresh
    parsley*
1 cup Garlic Croutons (page 208)

➣ Dredge the oysters in the cornmeal and set aside. (Save any liquid from the shucked oysters for stock.)

➣ Rinse and dry the spinach, remove any large stems, and tear into pieces; set aside.

➣ Cook the bacon in a large skillet until crisp. Remove the bacon from the pan and transfer it to brown paper or a paper towel to drain. Add the onion to the hot bacon fat and cook over medium heat just until wilted—do not let the onion brown or become crisp. Add the grated apple and continue cooking until it becomes completely soft, about 1 minute. Add the sugar, vinegar, wine, dry mustard, salt, and pepper. Stir well and continue cooking for about 1 minute, or until the sugar is dissolved. Turn off the heat.

➣ In another large skillet melt the butter over medium-high heat. Add the oysters, without crowding the pan, and cook until golden on both sides. This will take about 2 minutes per side. As they are done, transfer to an ovenproof plate and place in a warm oven.

To assemble the salad:

✒ Place the spinach in a large salad bowl. Crumble the bacon and add to the spinach, along with the cheese, walnuts, and parsley. Toss to combine. Pour the warm onion/apple/vinegar mixture over the spinach and toss. Add the croutons, toss again, and divide among the 4 serving plates. Place an equal portion of cooked oysters on each serving of spinach salad. Serve immediately.

SEARED SCALLOPS AND BABY GREENS SALAD

This salad is the heart of simplicity, but that's all that's needed here for stunning flavors.

Make the vinaigrette first and have the greens ready so that the salad can be served as soon as the scallops are seared.

Serves 4

Vinaigrette:

2 tablespoons fresh lemon juice

½ teaspoon Dijon mustard

½ teaspoon sugar

⅓ cup olive oil

1½ teaspoons chopped fresh parsley

1½ teaspoons chopped fresh chives

1½ teaspoons chopped fresh basil

Salt and pepper to taste

Salad:

4 cups mixed baby greens

1 cup fresh corn kernels

½ cup grated carrot

12 cherry tomatoes, halved

1 tablespoon olive oil

1 pound shucked scallops

✒ To make the vinaigrette, whisk together all ingredients in a bowl. Set aside.

✒ Toss the mixed baby greens in a bowl with the corn, carrot, and cherry tomatoes. Set aside.

✎ Place the oil in a large, heavy skillet over medium heat. When hot but not smoking, add the scallops and cook, turning with tongs, until they have a golden crust. As they are done, transfer to a platter.

✎ Divide the tossed greens among 4 plates. Top with the warm, seared scallops and pour the dressing over. Serve immediately.

SHRIMP, CORN, AND BLACK BEAN SALAD

This salad consists of jumbo shrimp panfried with a crisp cornmeal coating atop black beans, fresh uncooked corn, red pepper, and scallions—a fabulous combination of tastes, textures, and colors. I got the idea from a wonderful salad I had at El Mirador Restaurant in San Antonio, Texas. A cilantro dressing finishes the dish.

Four jumbo shrimp are allowed per person, which seems to be just right for a lunch dish. If you are serving this as a main course for dinner, you may want to increase the shrimp to five per person. If you like, place tomato wedges and avocado slices around each serving of salad.

The black beans will need to be soaked overnight before cooking. Both of these steps (soaking and cooking) can be done a day or two in advance.

Serves 6

For the vegetable salad:

2½ cups fresh corn kernels	*⅓ cup loosely packed chopped fresh cilantro*
2 cups cooked black beans, drained and completely cooled	*1 teaspoon salt*
	½ teaspoon freshly ground black pepper
¾ cup chopped scallion	*1 head romaine lettuce*
½ cup chopped red bell pepper	*½ cup Cilantro Dressing (see page 204)*

For the shrimp:

24 jumbo shrimp   Pinch of salt and pepper
¼ cup buttermilk   2 tablespoons olive oil
1 egg   2 tablespoons butter
1 cup yellow cornmeal

To make the salad:

✄ Combine the corn, beans, scallion, red pepper, cilantro, salt, and pepper in a large bowl. Toss well, cover, and refrigerate.

✄ Wash the lettuce and dry in a spinner or with paper towels. Wrap loosely with slightly damp paper towels and place in the crisper drawer of the refrigerator.

To prepare the shrimp:

✄ Shell and devein the shrimp, leaving the tails intact, then set aside. (Save the shrimp shells for stock.) Place the buttermilk in a small bowl. Place the egg in a separate small bowl and beat with a fork. In another bowl combine the cornmeal with the salt and pepper.

✄ In a large cast-iron skillet heat 1 tablespoon of oil and 1 tablespoon of butter over medium heat.

✄ Dip each shrimp in the buttermilk, in the cornmeal, in the beaten egg, and then in the cornmeal again. Press the shrimp into the cornmeal each time so that a good layer adheres to it. Place 12 of the shrimp in the hot pan, being careful not to crowd them, and cook until golden on each side, about 1 or 2 minutes per side. Turn with tongs once during the cooking process. As the shrimp are cooked, remove them to a plate lined with brown paper or paper towel. Repeat this process with the remaining oil and butter for the last 12 shrimp.

To assemble the salad:

✄ Pour the cilantro dressing over the vegetables and toss, thoroughly coating the salad ingredients. Let sit while you tear the lettuce into bite-size pieces and place an equal amount on each dinner plate. Top the lettuce with a mound of vegetable salad. Arrange 4 shrimp on the top. Serve immediately.

Skate, Often Overlooked

In the United States skate is one of those underutilized fish, while in Europe it has long been popular, especially in France and England. Its status here is about to change, as cod and other more traditionally popular fish become less available and more expensive.

Skate, or raja as it is sometimes called, is plentiful and inexpensive. If you don't see it at your fish market, ask for it. Chances are they are selling it wholesale to processors or restaurants. And the more often skate is requested, the more likely it will become a regular item in the retail display.

If you have never seen skate, it looks a lot like a manta ray, but smaller. The "wings" are the part of the fish that is used, and each wing provides two beautiful meaty fillets—four fillets per fish. I prefer the smaller skate, the four fillets equaling a total of about 1 pound.

If possible, buy skate that has been skinned and filleted. If not, see the directions on page 214.

SKATE AND FRENCH LENTIL SALAD

It is important to the success of this recipe that you use French lentils. They are smaller than the dried lentils most often used for soup, and they stand up well to cooking, holding their shape and not splitting or becoming mushy.

This salad must be made in advance. Unlike most dried beans, the lentils do not have to be soaked overnight, but the finished dish must be chilled for at least two hours before serving.

Serves 4

2¼ cups dried French lentils
   (Dean & DeLuca is a good brand)
2 cups water
1 tablespoon butter
1 pound skate fillets
1 cup diced tomato
½ cup chopped red onion
1 clove garlic, pressed

2 tablespoons finely chopped
   fresh parsley
3 tablespoons fresh lemon juice
1 tablespoon olive oil
¼ teaspoon salt
¼ teaspoon freshly ground black pepper
1 head red and green lettuce
1 lemon, cut into wedges

⁂ Place the lentils and water in a pot and bring to a boil, uncovered. When the water reaches a boil, lower the heat, cover the pot, and cook for approximately 20 minutes. The lentils should be tender but not mushy, so check them a couple of times during the cooking process. When done, pour off the cooking liquid (save for vegetable stock, if desired) and let the lentils cool in a colander.

⁂ Melt the butter in a large skillet over medium heat. Add the skate fillets and cook until golden on both sides, about 2 to 3 minutes per side. As the skate cooks, the fillets will separate into long narrow "fingers"; that's fine because they will be tossed with the other salad ingredients. The more golden the fish is, the better flavor it will add to the salad. When the skate is completely cooked, transfer it to a plate to cool.

⁂ When the lentils have *completely* cooled, place them in a large bowl. Add the tomato, onion, garlic, and parsley, and toss. Add the lemon juice, olive oil, salt, and pepper, and toss gently again.

⁂ Cut the skate into 1-inch sections. Add the skate and any juices from the plate to the lentil mixture. Toss gently, cover, and refrigerate for at least 2 hours. Bring to room temperature before serving.

⁂ To serve, place a few leaves of lettuce on each plate and top with salad. Serve with lemon wedges.

5

Pasta

Mending the net, 1990s—part of the never-ending shoreside work of fishing.

"The younger generation doesn't know twine because they don't have to. We had to build our own nets. We could build a complete net, four guys, in two and a half days. Took a lot of time."

—a fisherman

The last few years have seen pasta become one of the most popular foods in America. When my generation was growing up, pasta (a word no one even used then) meant spaghetti with a thick red tomato sauce, but nowadays we know the difference between linguine, fettuccine, and angel-hair pasta, and we love the versatility of this humble food.

Another reason for pasta's huge popularity is our recent recognition of it as a healthful way to eat. Pasta is a low-fat, high-carbohydrate food. And meals where pasta is the main course generally contain more carbohydrate and fiber than meat, which we now know is a very good way to eat.

When that meat portion is seafood, you have a combination that not only is healthful but sublimely delicious. In this chapter you'll find eleven different recipes for pasta dishes using all kinds of seafood. You can use rather small amounts of some of the more expensive seafoods, such as lobster, with stunning results, or the seafood can be left over from the previous day's meal. And for variety, any of these sauces can be served over rice instead of pasta.

The Best Way to Cook Pasta

Bring a large pot of lightly salted cold water to a boil. Add the pasta (noodles or ravioli) and keep them from sticking together by stirring gently with a wooden spoon while the water returns to a boil. Continue to cook, uncovered, until done. This is about 4 minutes for fresh pasta and between 8 and 12 minutes for boxed pasta (the package will have a suggested cooking time). Test for doneness, drain, and serve.

FETTUCCINE WITH SCALLOPS IN A ROSEMARY CREAM SAUCE

A golden brown, rosemary-flavored cream sauce gives this dish a flavor well suited for fall and winter. Once you have the ingredients at hand, the sauce can be assembled in the time it takes to cook the pasta.

This is very good served with Stewed Swiss Chard (page 170).

Serves 4

3 tablespoons butter
1 pound shucked scallops
3 tablespoons finely minced shallots
2 cloves garlic, finely minced
1 cup dry white wine, such as a chardonnay
1 pound tomato fettuccine (or plain fettuccine if tomato is unavailable)
1 teaspoon finely chopped fresh rosemary
1 cup light cream
2 tablespoons grated Parmesan cheese
Salt and pepper to taste
1 tablespoon finely chopped fresh parsley

Melt 2 tablespoons of butter in a large skillet over medium heat. Add the scallops and cook them, turning them carefully with tongs, until they are golden on all sides. As they are cooked, remove them to a plate, and cover. When all the scallops have been cooked, add the shallots and garlic to the pan and cook over medium heat until tender and fragrant. Add the wine, stirring to scrape the garlic and shallots from the bottom of the pan. Cook until the wine is reduced by half.

While the wine is reducing, bring a large pot of lightly salted cold water to a boil. When the sauce is nearly complete, cook the pasta (see page 82).

Add the rosemary to the reduced wine sauce, stirring quickly, and then pour in the cream. Lower the heat slightly, then whisk in the remaining tablespoon of butter and the

L. A. Dunton *on the fishing grounds with crew aft baiting up trawls.*

The *L. A. Dunton* was built in Essex, Massachusetts, in 1921, and is one of the last surviving examples of an American fishing schooner—boats renowned worldwide for their speed and beauty. After a long career as a fishing vessel and then a coastal freighter, the *Dunton* is now the property of Mystic Seaport (in Mystic, Connecticut), where she is docked and available for the public to view and tour.

Parmesan cheese. Pour in the liquid that has formed on the plate with the scallops, stir, and season with salt and pepper to taste. Add the scallops and turn the heat to the lowest setting; keep the skillet partially covered.

✎ Place the cooked and drained fettuccine in a large pasta serving bowl. Spoon the scallops and sauce over all, sprinkle with parsley, toss, and serve.

LINGUINE WITH LOBSTER SAUCE

This recipe can be produced quickly and is a delicious way to use lobster meat left over from a steamed lobster dinner. A small amount of lobster goes a long way. Add a green salad and Italian bread, and you have a memorable meal.

You can substitute lump crabmeat for the lobster.

Serves 4

2 tablespoons olive oil

1 tablespoon butter

2 cloves garlic, minced

2 tablespoons minced shallots

2 cups coarsely chopped cooked lobster meat (about 1 pound)

4 tablespoons cognac

2 cups peeled and chopped plum tomatoes

1 cup dry white wine

2 teaspoons finely chopped fresh tarragon or basil

Salt and pepper to taste

1 pound linguine, cooked al dente (see page 82)

4 tablespoons grated Parmesan cheese

✎ Heat the olive oil and butter in a large skillet. Add the garlic and shallots, and cook over medium heat until tender and translucent but not browned. Add the lobster meat and continue to cook for another 2 minutes. Pour in the cognac and light with a match. When the flame dies, add the tomatoes, wine, and herbs. Bring to a simmer, stir, cover partially, and cook over low heat for 5 minutes. Add salt and pepper to taste.

Toss the cooked and drained pasta with the Parmesan cheese. Put a serving of pasta on individual plates and top with lobster sauce. Serve immediately.

Variation:

To make this a creamy sauce, add ½ cup of light cream to the mixture after the tomatoes, wine, and herbs have simmered for 5 minutes. Continue to heat until the mixture returns to a simmer, and add salt and pepper to taste.

LINGUINE WITH WHITE CLAM SAUCE

Buy fresh littleneck clams or fresh small quahogs if you have the time to steam them and pick the meat; otherwise, buy canned baby clams. Starting with clams in the shell provides you with a flavorful broth and the best results.

This sauce can be refrigerated and served the next day.

Serves 4 to 6

1½ cups clam meat; if using fresh clams in the shell, about 18 small quahogs or 24 littlenecks will produce this yield

¼ cup olive oil

2 tablespoons butter

¼ cup minced celery

¼ cup minced onion

3 cloves garlic, pressed

1 tablespoon unbleached flour

1 tablespoon light cream

½ cup dry white wine

1 cup clam broth

⅓ cup finely chopped fresh parsley

1½ pounds linguine, cooked al dente (see page 82)

½ cup grated Parmesan cheese for topping

To cook the clams:

If you are using fresh clams in the shell, follow the directions on page 142 and reserve 1 cup of the broth, strained, for this recipe.

To make the sauce:

Heat the olive oil and butter in a large, heavy skillet over medium heat. Add the celery, onion, and garlic, and cook, stirring occasionally, until tender but not browned. Sprinkle in the flour and stir until it is incorporated. Add the cream, stirring until it is blended and the cream and flour are thick. Add the wine, stir, and cook until the wine is blended with the cream sauce. Add the clam broth and stir. Lower the heat and allow to simmer, partially covered, for 10 minutes.

Add the clams and parsley to the sauce. Stir, cover, and keep over the lowest heat while you drain the pasta.

Place a portion of pasta on each dinner plate and top with a generous spoonful of clam sauce. Top with some grated Parmesan cheese. Serve immediately.

Seafood Is Not Free for the Taking

Visiting a New England fishing port on a fair day at the beginning of summer can be a real treat. The warmth of the sun after a long cold winter, the sound of the water lapping against the sides of the boats, and fresh salty smells soothe the soul and whet the appetite.

At the end of the day when the lobster boats come in, you're likely to find the fishermen selling some of their catch at the dock. It doesn't get any fresher than this, and the price is a bargain, too. It's fun taking part in the transactions, and this lively exchange becomes part of the excitement of the feast to come.

But as you haggle over price, remember that for the fisherman, lobsters are not free. Lobstermen make enormous investments to go fishing; today in New England it is not unusual for a lobsterman with a "day boat" to have a sizable boat mortgage ($50,000 to $100,000 is not uncommon), and gear in the water—traps, line, buoys—can run to $40,000. Then there's boat and crew insurance, dockage, fuel, and a crew to pay before the lobsterman sees a dime. Something to remember.

SPAGHETTINI WITH MUSSELS DIJON

Spaghettini is slightly more delicate than linguine but not quite as fine as angel-hair pasta. When there are more noodles per pound of pasta, more surface area is created for the sauce, and its thinness lends a more tender texture to each bite.

In this recipe the distinct flavor of mussels is enhanced with an herbed mustard sauce. The herb here is tarragon, but you can easily substitute thyme or another favorite.

Mussels vary in size. If the shells are all approximately 3 inches in length, you will need about 4 pounds to yield enough meat for this recipe. If the shells are smaller, you'll need about 5 pounds.

Serves 4 to 6

> *4 pounds live mussels (shells of 3-inch*
> *size), scrubbed and debearded*
> *1½ pounds spaghettini, cooked al dente*
> *(see page 82)*

For the sauce:

½ cup olive oil
¼ cup finely chopped shallots
1 clove garlic, pressed
½ cup dry white wine
1 cup mussel broth
1 tablespoon fresh lemon juice
½ teaspoon anchovy paste
3 tablespoons Dijon mustard

1 tablespoon light cream
2 teaspoons finely chopped fresh
tarragon
1 tablespoon finely chopped fresh
parsley
¼ teaspoon freshly ground black
pepper
Grated Parmesan cheese for topping

To cook the mussels:

⌇ Clean, cook, and pick the mussels according to the directions on page 142, reserving 1 cup of the mussel broth for this recipe.

To make the sauce:

✑ Place the oil in a large, heavy skillet and heat over medium heat. When the oil is hot, add the shallots and garlic, and cook until fragrant but not browned. Add the wine, mussel broth, and lemon juice, and stir. When the mixture returns to a simmer, add the anchovy paste. Stir in the mustard, cream, herbs, and black pepper. Lower the heat and allow to simmer, partially covered, for 5 minutes. Add the mussels. Cover and keep over the lowest heat while you drain the pasta.

✑ Spoon a portion of mussels and sauce over each serving of spaghettini. Serve immediately.

ANGEL-HAIR PASTA WITH SHRIMP, PEAS, AND DILL

I developed this recipe for Maine shrimp, but small or medium Gulf shrimp work well, too, since Maine shrimp are available fresh only a few months of the year.
Serves 4

3 tablespoons butter	*2 teaspoons chopped fresh dill*
½ cup finely diced onion	*1½ pounds shrimp, uncooked and*
½ cup finely diced carrot	*cleaned*
2 tablespoons flour	*1½ cups peas*
2¼ cups milk	*1 pound angel-hair pasta*
¼ cup dry white wine	*Salt and pepper to taste*
2 tablespoons chopped fresh parsley	

✑ In a large, heavy skillet melt the butter over medium heat. Cook the onion and carrot until tender. Sprinkle in the flour and stir until it is incorporated. Add the milk slowly, stirring constantly and allowing the sauce to thicken after each addition, until all the milk is added and the sauce is thick. Add the wine and continue cooking to thicken again. Add the herbs, shrimp, peas, salt and pepper. Stir gently and keep on the lowest heat for about 10 minutes. In the meantime, add the angel-hair pasta to a pot of boiling water. When the pasta is cooked al dente, drain and transfer it to a wide, shallow bowl. Top with the shrimp sauce, toss, and serve immediately.

ANGEL-HAIR PASTA WITH SMOKED SALMON CARBONARA

I kept trying to come up with a sauce for pasta using *poached* salmon, and each time I was unhappy with the results. Then it dawned on me: "Why not make a carbonara-style sauce using *smoked* salmon instead of pancetta?" We love it. I hope you will, too. As you'll see, a little smoked salmon goes a long way. Angel hair is a good pasta for this.
Serves 4

1 tablespoon olive oil

1 tablespoon butter

2 medium onions, thinly sliced

½ pound smoked salmon, sliced in
  ¼-inch pieces

2 cups milk

2 tablespoons white wine vinegar

1 pound angel-hair pasta, cooked
  al dente (see page 82)

1 cup blanched peas

1 egg, beaten

¼ cup grated Parmesan cheese

2 tablespoons chopped fresh dill

Freshly ground black pepper to taste

In a large, heavy skillet heat the oil and butter over medium heat. When hot, add the onion slices. Lower the heat, cover, and cook for 15 minutes, or until the onions are completely tender and translucent but not browned. Lift the lid occasionally and stir. Add the salmon and continue cooking for 1 minute. Add the milk, bring to a simmer, and cook for 4 minutes. Add the vinegar. At this point the mixture will separate, but don't despair—you have not ruined it. Continue to cook the mixture at a low simmer for about 15 minutes, stirring occasionally, and it will become smooth again.

✎ While the mixture is simmering, cook the pasta and drain well. As soon as you drain the pasta, add the peas to the salmon sauce.

✎ Transfer the drained pasta to a pasta bowl or return to the pot in which it was cooked. Add to the pasta the beaten egg, Parmesan cheese, dill, and pepper, and toss well to coat thoroughly.

✎ Pour the salmon sauce over the cooked, drained, and seasoned pasta. Toss gently to combine and serve immediately.

A dragger sails out of New Bedford.

During the 1980s, New Bedford was the nation's most profitable fishing port. This was due not only to the size of the fleet and catches but also because of the high quantities of scallops and yellowtail flounder in the total landings, both of which command very high prices.

LINGUINE WITH SQUID

This sauce is flavored with sun-dried tomatoes, sweet red peppers, and a little Madeira wine, all pulled together with a splash of light cream. The squid is lightly sautéed before it becomes part of the sauce, giving it more flavor and a tender texture.
Serves 4

1½ pounds cleaned squid (see page 25)	*½ cup light cream*
1 cup sun-dried tomatoes	*4 tablespoons chopped fresh parsley*
3 tablespoons olive oil	*4 tablespoons chopped fresh basil*
¼ cup julienned red bell pepper	*2 tablespoons Madeira wine*
½ cup thinly sliced onion	*1 pound linguine, cooked al dente*
4 cloves garlic, minced	*(see page 82)*

≫ Cut the squid bodies into rings about ¼ inch thick. Leave the tentacles whole, or if they are very large, halve them. Set aside.

≫ Cut the sun-dried tomatoes in quarters and put in a bowl. Add enough boiling water to just cover and let them sit for 15 minutes. Drain, reserving ¼ cup of the liquid for the sauce. Set aside.

≫ Place the oil in a large, heavy skillet over medium heat. When hot, add the squid. Cook, stirring, for about 1 minute, or until the squid begins to turn opaque white. Add the red pepper, onion, garlic, and sun-dried tomatoes, and continue cooking over medium heat until the vegetables are tender but not browned, about 2 minutes. Add the cream, herbs, wine, and ¼ cup of reserved liquid from the sun-dried tomatoes. Stir and continue cooking until the sauce is thoroughly heated.

≫ Drain the linguine, pour the sauce over the hot drained linguine, toss, and serve.

The Best Commercial Lasagna

If you are not going to make your own lasagna noodles, use the Ondine brand available in most supermarkets and gourmet shops. They are thin, delicate noodles that do *not* need to be cooked before assembling the lasagna, and they are the closest thing to fresh-from-scratch I've found.

Each package includes two 8-inch-square baking pans and enough noodles for two generous lasagnas.

SHRIMP LASAGNA

Seven delicate layers of noodles are filled with spinach, cheeses, a little tomato sauce, and lots of fresh shrimp. This freezes well.

Serves 6 (makes one 8-inch-square lasagna)

*1 box frozen spinach, thawed and well
    drained*
2 eggs, beaten
2 cloves garlic, crushed
1 pound ricotta cheese
¼ cup grated Parmesan cheese
¼ cup packed fresh basil leaves
½ cup grated mozzarella cheese

¼ cup goat cheese
2 cups marinara sauce
*1 package Ondine lasagna noodles
    (you'll use only 7) or sufficient fresh
    pasta sheets to make 7 layers*
*1 pound medium shrimp, uncooked,
    shelled, and deveined*

Preheat oven to 350 degrees.

⤳ Place the spinach, eggs, garlic, ricotta and Parmesan cheeses, basil, ¼ cup of mozzarella, and goat cheese in a food processor fitted with the metal blade. Pulse until ingredients are well combined. Transfer to a large bowl and stir in 1½ cups of marinara sauce.

⤳ Pour ¼ cup of the remaining marinara sauce in the bottom of an 8-inch by 8-inch lasagna pan. Cover with a sheet of lasagna noodles. Spread ⅔ cup of the spinach/cheese mixture on the noodles. Lay ⅙ of the cleaned shrimp over the spinach/cheese mixture and top with a sheet of lasagna noodles. Repeat this process until you have used up all the noodles and all the filling and shrimp. End with a layer of lasagna noodles. Pour the remaining ¼ cup of marinara sauce over the top and sprinkle with the remaining ¼ cup of mozzarella cheese. Cover the pan with foil and bake in the oven for 30 minutes. Remove the foil and bake 15 minutes more.

⤳ Remove to a cooling rack and let sit, covered with a *loose* foil tent, for 15 minutes. Cut into squares and serve.

SPINACH AND GOAT CHEESE RAVIOLI

This is a great basic ravioli to pair with nearly any seafood sauce. It is strongly flavored with spinach, basil, and goat cheese, and makes an absolutely perfect partner to the Light Cream Sauce with Shrimp that follows.

You can buy fresh ravioli sheets at gourmet shops. Ravioli plaques that help you form and fill the ravioli are also available in specialty stores and gourmet shops, such as Williams-Sonoma.

Makes about 36 ravioli

1 cup packed fresh spinach leaves	*1 tablespoon ricotta cheese*
2 tablespoons chopped fresh basil	*Salt and pepper to taste*
½ teaspoon minced fresh garlic	*6 ravioli sheets, approximately*
1 teaspoon minced shallot	*5 inches by 16 inches*
1 cup goat cheese	

To make the filling:

Place the spinach, basil, garlic, and shallot in a blender and pulse until pureed. Transfer to a bowl. Using a fork, mash the goat cheese into the spinach puree until thoroughly blended. Do not do this in the blender because the mixture will become too soupy. Stir in the ricotta and add salt and pepper to taste.

To make the ravioli:

Stack the sheets of ravioli dough between sheets of wax paper and cover with a clean damp dish towel to keep them from drying out while you fill and form the ravioli.

Lightly sprinkle the ravioli plaque with a little semolina flour. Lay a sheet of pasta over it and use your knuckle to make a slight depression in the pasta over each ravioli indentation, being careful not to tear the pasta. Fill each indentation with a heaping teaspoon of filling. Use your finger or a small brush to moisten the edges of each ravioli with a little water. Drape another sheet of pasta over this and pat it down gently with your hand, carefully pressing out air bubbles. (Air bubbles in the ravioli can cause them to burst when cooking, thus losing the filling.)

Press a rolling pin slowly and firmly across the plaque to cut the ravioli. Invert the plaque onto a lightly floured board and lift it away from the ravioli. If the ravioli have not all separated from one another, use a knife or pizza wheel to cut through the perforations made by the raised ridges in the plaque.

Set the ravioli aside on a lightly floured plate or board until ready to cook. Repeat the process until all the filling is used. You should have about 3 dozen ravioli.

Bring a large pot of lightly salted water to a boil. Carefully slip the ravioli into the water and cook, uncovered, for about 4 minutes, or until tender. Remove the ravioli from the water with a slotted spoon and place gently in a colander to drain before serving.

It's no fish ye're buying — it's men's lives.

—Sir Walter Scott, *The Antiquary*

A LIGHT CREAM SAUCE WITH SHRIMP FOR RAVIOLI

Because ravioli are rich and more filling than pasta noodles, this sauce is light on the seafood. You can increase the amount if you wish, but I think you'll find this to be just right. A couple of ravioli with a spoonful of this sauce makes an elegant first course.
Serves 4

2 tablespoons butter	*½ cup milk*
½ pound medium shrimp, uncooked,	*2 teaspoons goat cheese*
peeled, and deveined	*¼ cup chopped and drained stewed*
1 tablespoon finely chopped onion	*tomatoes*
¼ cup dry white wine	*1 teaspoon chopped fresh basil*
1 tablespoon unbleached flour	*Salt and pepper to taste*

⊱ In a large, heavy, lightly oiled skillet, melt the butter over medium heat. Add the shrimp and cook until they are pink with golden edges. Remove the shrimp with a slotted spoon and transfer to a plate. Add the onion to the skillet and cook until tender and translucent but not browned. Add the wine and cook until the liquid is slightly reduced. Sprinkle in the flour and stir until it is incorporated. Slowly add the milk, whisking after each addition, until the mixture is slightly thickened. Stir in the goat cheese, and when it is melted, add the tomatoes and basil. Season to taste with salt and pepper. Return the shrimp to the pan, along with any juices that have formed on the plate, and keep over medium-low heat until the sauce is thoroughly heated.

⊱ The sauce can be put over ravioli such as the Spinach and Goat Cheese Ravioli (page 93) or any other filled ravioli.

LOBSTER AND ASPARAGUS PASTA SALAD

Lobster meat, cherry tomatoes, and asparagus spears make a pretty and flavorful salad with tender small pasta shells, blended with a classic vinaigrette. This is as appropriate for dinner as it is for a special picnic.

Serves 4 to 6

For the salad:

1 pound cooked lobster meat,
  coarsely chopped
12 cherry tomatoes, quartered
1 pound tender asparagus, blanched
  and cut in 1-inch pieces

2 cups small pasta shells, cooked
  al dente (see page 82)
1 head Boston lettuce

For the vinaigrette:

⅓ cup olive oil
1 teaspoon Dijon mustard
1 teaspoon honey
2 tablespoons white wine vinegar
1 tablespoon fresh lemon juice

½ teaspoon chopped fresh tarragon
1 teaspoon chopped fresh parsley
1 teaspoon chopped fresh chives
Salt and pepper to taste

➤ In a large bowl combine all the salad ingredients except the lettuce. Toss gently.

➤ In a separate bowl whisk together the vinaigrette ingredients. Pour over the salad and toss. Allow to sit for 10 minutes.

➤ Arrange some lettuce on each plate. Toss the salad again and spoon a portion on each lettuce bed. Serve immediately.

SCALLOP AND PESTO PASTA SALAD

This meal-in-one dish is a good summer recipe, especially if you have a vegetable garden. Shrimp, grilled tuna, or grilled monkfish could be substituted for the scallops.

This salad can be made in advance, which allows the flavors to develop.

Serves 6

1 large eggplant, diced (unpeeled)
(about 8 cups)
3 tablespoons olive oil
¼ teaspoon salt
3 sweet red bell peppers, roasted
(see page 209)
1 pound shucked scallops

1 tablespoon butter
1 pound small pasta shells
1 cup Basic Pesto (see page 206)
¼ cup light cream
2½ cups diced plum tomatoes
3 tablespoons finely chopped fresh
parsley

Preheat oven to 400 degrees.

Place the eggplant in a large shallow pan and sprinkle with 2 tablespoons of olive oil and the salt. Toss to coat evenly. Bake for approximately 35 minutes, turning with a spatula once or twice during baking. The eggplant should not be mushy. Cool on a rack.

Cut the peppers into thin slices, about ¼ inch by 1 inch. Set aside on a plate.

Heat the remaining tablespoon of olive oil and the butter in a large skillet over medium heat. Place the scallops in the skillet and sear them, turning them with tongs as they cook, until they are golden on all sides. When completely cooked, remove to a plate along with any juices that have formed in the pan and set aside.

Bring a large pot of lightly salted water to a boil and cook the pasta. While it is cooking, prepare the pesto and combine it with the light cream in a small bowl. When the pasta is cooked, drain it and transfer it to a large bowl. Spoon the pesto mixture over the pasta while it is still warm and toss well. Set aside to cool to room temperature.

Add the roasted eggplant, red peppers, scallops, tomatoes, and parsley to the pasta, including any juices that have formed on the plate with the scallops and peppers. Toss gently. Cover and let sit for at least 30 minutes. Serve at room temperature.

Main Course—Finfish

Dory fishing for cod, 1920s.

During Gloucester's fishing schooner heyday, most of the fish brought in from the "banks" (either Georges Bank or the Grand Banks) was caught by men in dories with trawls. Dory fishing was done year-round on the open ocean from flat-bottomed boats of about 15 feet in length. Two men per dory was standard, and once the fishing vessel had reached the grounds, they were launched over the side to row a mile or two away to set their trawls—lines with baited hooks. Trawls were kept in half barrels and had an anchor on one end and a buoy on the other. It was not unusual for a dory to return to the ship with almost 1,000 pounds of fish, which then had to be gutted, dressed, and salted.

In the two sections of this chapter you will find more than two dozen ways to prepare fish and shellfish. (You can also find good main-course recipe ideas in the chapters on Chowders, Bisques, Soups, and Stews; Salads; Pasta; and Pizzas.)

I start with simple and basic techniques for baking, sautéing, and grilling fish. These are *always* good ways to treat fresh fish—you can't go wrong with plain and simple. Beyond that are recipes for roasted whole fish, fish casseroles, pan-seared, baked, broiled, or stuffed fillets, and steaks that can be grilled whole or cubed for the stir-fry pan or skewers. Some recipes are quite plain, while others include sauces made with herbs, vegetables, wine, and cream.

Virtually every fish available in New England markets is used here, and nearly every recipe includes suggestions for substitutions.

I've specifically called for some fish here that you may never have tried. Tilefish, sea trout (weakfish), and tautog (blackfish) are delicious and relatively unknown. And if you never have, you must try mackerel, an unfairly maligned fish that is delicious, cheap, highly available, and the best source of Omega-3 fatty acids—excellent for the heart.

So dive in and have some fun. Experiment. Tell yourself that you will try at least one new fish a month, and stick to it. You and your family will be well rewarded for the effort.

Determining How Much Fish to Buy

A whole fish will generally yield about half its weight in fillets. For instance, a 2-pound flounder will yield about 1 pound of fillets.

Three to 4 ounces of fish per person is usually good for a starter course, and 6 to 8 ounces is usually about right for a main-course serving.

BASIC BAKED FISH FILLETS

If you're short on time or ingredients, you can bake any fish fillet this way with wonderful results. This is easily doubled, and if you end up with a double layer of fillets, place the bottom layer skin side down in the pan, and the top layer skin side up. In that case, place a tablespoon of butter in the bottom of the baking pan and use half of the butter, lemon, and wine between the two layers and the other half on top.
Serves 2 to 4

1 pound fish fillets	*2 tablespoons fine plain bread crumbs*
2 tablespoons butter, melted	*1 tablespoon finely chopped*
2 tablespoons fresh lemon juice	* fresh parsley*
2 tablespoons dry white wine	*Lemon wedges*

➤ Preheat oven to 350 degrees.

➤ Spread half of the melted butter in a 9-inch by 13-inch ovenproof dish. Place the fish fillets, skin side down, in the dish in a single layer. Pour the remaining butter evenly over the fish, then the lemon juice and wine. Top with the bread crumbs and place in the oven for 20 minutes, or until the fish is completely cooked and piping hot. Serve immediately, adding some of the juices from the baking pan to each serving. Top each serving with a little of the fresh parsley and serve with lemon wedges.

Note: The thicker the fillets, the longer the baking time. Check with a fork for doneness. Undercooked fish does not have as much flavor as thoroughly cooked fish and does not have as flaky and tender a texture.

BASIC SAUTÉED FISH FILLETS

Fish fillets can be deliciously prepared with a quick sauté on top of the stove. I find a cast-iron skillet works best for this, but any good heavy-bottomed skillet will do fine.
Serves 2 to 4

⅓ cup unbleached flour	*1 pound fish fillets*
⅓ cup cornmeal	*1 tablespoon vegetable oil*
Salt and pepper to taste	*1 tablespoon butter*

➣ Combine the flour and cornmeal, seasoned with a little salt and pepper, in a wide, shallow bowl. Dredge the fish fillets in the mixture.

➣ Heat the oil and butter over medium heat in a large, heavy skillet. When hot but not smoking, add the fish fillets and cook, turning only once, until golden on both sides. (You will know when it is time to turn the fillets by the golden brown edges that appear as the meat becomes whiter and more opaque. If you flip a fillet a little too early, you'll know to give the others a little more time. A 4-ounce flounder fillet takes about 2 minutes per side.) Serve immediately.

Note: You can eliminate the flour dredge, but I think it helps to hold in some of the juices and flavor.

Grilling Whole Fish

Nearly any whole fish can be cooked on a grill. Always scale and gut the fish first; remove the gills and trim off any sharp fins. Rub the fish with oil, place in a grilling basket, and then set on the hot grill.

Sea bass, mackerel, sea trout, and other meaty fish with substantial skins are good choices for this kind of cooking. As the fish cooks, the skin holds in the moisture and flavor. When completely cooked, the fillets should lift off the bone easily.

BASIC GRILLED FISH STEAKS

Swordfish, tuna, and salmon steaks are wonderful when cooked perfectly plain over a bed of hot coals on an outdoor grill. (If you don't have a grill, you can use a grill pan on top of the stove.) Other firm-fleshed fish, such as monkfish, can also be cubed and skewered, or cut in medallions, and grilled. (See note that follows.) Any fish suitable for grilling can be marinated first to add flavor and to help keep the steaks moist.

Serves 4

> *2 pounds fish steaks, cut about 1 inch thick*
> *Lemon wedges*

Make sure the grilling rack is clean and dry, then give the side that the fish will sit on a light swipe of cooking oil. Set the rack about 6 to 8 inches above the hot coals.

Place the steaks on the rack when it is hot. (Test by flicking a little water at it; if it hisses, it is hot.)

⤛ Cook about 5 minutes per side (about 10 minutes cooking time per inch), flipping only once. The outside of the steaks should have a nicely seared "crust," and the inside should be completely cooked, piping hot, and juicy. When the steaks are done, immediately transfer to plates and serve. Lemon wedges are the only accompaniment needed.

Note: You can give the steaks a thin coating of mayonnaise before grilling, if desired, for an even juicier steak.

When grilling kebabs, always marinate seafood and vegetables separately. Baste the kebabs sparingly during the grilling; too much marinade will cause the charcoal to flame. If using bamboo skewers, soak them in cold water for about 15 minutes before threading the ingredients onto them. Kebabs cook faster than steaks; they may need only a few minutes.

Grilling Fish Fillets

Remember to remove the scales before filleting fish. Fish fillets generally cannot be successfully cooked directly on the grill. The meat becomes too flaky as it cooks and will fall apart (and into the coals) as you turn it. To prevent this, wrap the grill snugly with a layer of heavy-duty foil, oil it lightly, and then pierce it all over with a toothpick. When the grill is hot, lay the fillets on the foil. Be careful not to tear the foil when turning the fish.

Fillets with the skin on are especially good candidates for this technique. The skin acts as a net: It holds the meat together as it cooks, preserves the moisture, and adds flavor. Mackerel, bluefish, striped bass, and salmon are all good cooked this way.

PANFRIED FLOUNDER WITH LEMON AND WINE SAUCE

This is a classic dish, often called Flounder Française in Italian restaurants.

Even using a 12-inch skillet you may have to cook the fish in batches, but be sure to remove the fish as it is done. Transfer to a plate in a warm oven and return it to the pan to finish in the sauce.

This goes together quickly once the fish are in the pan so have the other parts of the dinner ready before you start cooking the fish.

Serves 4

3 eggs	*2 tablespoons olive oil*
4 tablespoons milk	*8 tablespoons butter*
1½ cups flour	*1 cup dry white wine*
Salt and pepper to taste	*1 cup fresh lemon juice*
2 pounds fish fillets: flounder, whiting,	*½ cup chopped fresh parsley*
tilefish, or hake	

➣ In a wide, shallow bowl beat the eggs with the milk. In a separate bowl mix the flour with a little salt and pepper. Dredge the fish in the flour, pressing well to coat, then dip in the egg mixture, and then back in the flour mixture, pressing well again. Set on a platter as they are done.

➣ In a heavy 12-inch skillet heat the oil and butter over medium heat. When it is hot but not smoking, place the fillets in the pan but do not crowd. Cook until golden. Turn once and cook until golden on the other side (about 2 minutes per side). As soon as the fish is done, add the wine and lemon juice to the pan. Cover, remove from the heat, and let sit for 5 minutes.

➣ To serve, place a portion of fillets on each plate. Top with sauce and fresh parsley. Serve immediately.

Incentive of the "Share"

Commercial fishermen earn a percentage of the catch, called a share. This means a trip can be boom or bust; there are no financial guarantees for captain or crew, another one of the uncertainties of this business. This system of pay is as old as fishing and is not likely to change. As Sterling Hayden so aptly observed, "How else could such a vast amount of raw work as goes on in the fisheries ever get done?"

SKATE WITH BLACK BUTTER AND CAPERS

This recipe is considered one of the classic preparations for skate and is from one of our favorite Rhode Island restaurants, Chez Pascal in Narragansett. The fish is poached, then topped with a sauce of browned butter with capers, wine vinegar, and fresh parsley. Simple but exquisitely flavorful.

For more information on skate, see page 76.

Serves 4

4 skate wings, equaling about 3 pounds	*Salt*
½ cup white vinegar	*8 tablespoons butter*
¼ teaspoon whole black peppercorns	*½ cup drained capers*
2 bay leaves	*2 tablespoons red wine vinegar*
2 sprigs of fresh thyme or	*4 tablespoons chopped fresh parsley*
½ teaspoon dried thyme	

To poach the fish:

✃ Put the skate wings in a large saucepan and add enough water to cover. Set over high heat, bring to a boil, then lower the heat and simmer for 2 minutes. Drain and place the skate in a pan of ice water to stop the cooking.

✃ When the skate is cool, pat it dry and place it on a work surface. Remove and discard the skin by scraping it off with a sharp knife. Lift the two fillets of each wing away from the

Sword fishing, summer, early 1980s.

Top left: Until recently swordfish were harpooned. Note the man on the narrow "pulpit," forward of the bow, holding harpoon. Two men in rigging are "spotters," helping guide the boat onto swordfish.

Top right: Even on the hottest summer day, the swordfish spotters had to bundle up to keep warm for the hours spent in the "hoops" 40 to 50 feet above the deck.

Bottom left: Pilots were often hired to help spot schools of swordfish. It was dangerous work (this photo was taken by a man in the rigging) as the flying was done low and far out to sea.

Bottom right: The long hours and hard work pay off when a big swordfish like this one is landed. Photo taken by spotter in hoops above deck.

cartilage that separates them. Discard the cartilage, leaving the fillets intact, especially at the top edge.

⚬ Place the fillets in a saucepan or 2 that will hold them in a single layer. Add enough water to cover and then add the white vinegar, peppercorns, bay leaves, thyme, and a pinch of salt. Place the saucepan over medium heat and bring to a gentle simmer. Turn off the heat and let the fillets sit for 4 minutes. Use a slotted spatula to transfer them to a warm platter.

To make the sauce:

⚬ Melt the butter in a skillet set over medium-high heat, swirling it around the pan until it is dark brown. Add the capers and wine vinegar. Shake the pan to blend the ingredients, then immediately pour the sauce over the fillets. Sprinkle with parsley and serve immediately.

PAN-SEARED SEA TROUT WITH TOMATOES AND HERBS

A quick flash in sesame oil before being baked slowly in the oven with stewed tomatoes and herbs gives this fish an outstanding flavor. Other fish can be substituted for the sea trout — cod, haddock, or hake would be excellent.

Serves 4

2 pounds sea trout fillets
4 tablespoons fresh lemon juice
4 tablespoons sesame oil
1 cup finely chopped onion
4 cloves garlic, pressed
3 cups stewed tomatoes, drained
* and chopped*
4 tablespoons chopped fresh
* flat-leaf parsley*

2 tablespoons vinegar
2 tablespoons dry red wine
¼ teaspoon salt
1 teaspoon chopped fresh
* marjoram*
½ teaspoon chopped fresh thyme
2 teaspoons sugar
⅓ cup water

⋙ Preheat oven to 300 degrees.

⋙ Place the fillets in a wide, shallow glass dish and pour the lemon juice over them. Turn so that both sides have juice on them.

⋙ Place the sesame oil in a large, heavy skillet over medium heat. When hot but not smoking, add the fish and cook for 1 minute on each side. Remove and transfer to a wide, shallow baking dish.

⋙ In the same oil, over medium heat, cook the onion, garlic, and tomatoes for 5 minutes, stirring occasionally. Add the parsley, vinegar, wine, salt, marjoram, thyme, sugar, and water. Cook for another 5 minutes.

⋙ Pour the sauce over the fish and place in the middle of the oven. Bake for 20 minutes. Serve immediately.

CRISPY HERBED TAUTOG WITH HONEY MUSTARD BUTTER

A coating of white cornmeal, rolled oats, and herbs makes a crisp, handsome shell for the fillets. When served, they are topped with beautiful little disks of an herbed honey mustard butter, which covers the fish as the butter melts—a stunning presentation for a dinner party. Make the honey mustard butter first; it has to chill for at least thirty minutes before using.

This recipe is an adaptation of one from Nancy Carr, the former chef at The South Shore Grille, Wakefield, Rhode Island.

Serves 6

For the honey mustard butter:

> *6 tablespoons butter, softened*
> *1 tablespoon Dijon mustard*
> *2 tablespoons honey*
> *2 tablespoons finely chopped fresh parsley*

For the egg wash:

> *2 eggs*
> *2 tablespoons water*
> *¼ teaspoon cayenne pepper*
> *2 tablespoons Dijon mustard*
> *Pinch of salt and pepper*

For the crispy coating:

> *1 cup johnnycake meal (white cornmeal)*   *1 teaspoon dried marjoram*
> *½ cup rolled oats*   *¼ teaspoon salt*
> *1 teaspoon dried thyme*   *¼ teaspoon freshly ground black pepper*
> *1 teaspoon dried basil*
>
> *3 pounds tautog fillets*
> *2 tablespoons vegetable oil*
> *2 tablespoons butter*
>
> *12 lemon wedges*

To make the honey mustard butter:

Combine the softened butter, mustard, honey, and parsley in a bowl and beat together until thoroughly blended. Transfer to plastic wrap and form into a long log about 1 inch in diameter. Chill in the refrigerator for 1 hour or in the freezer for 30 minutes, until completely firm.

For the fillets:

Prepare the egg wash: In a wide, shallow bowl beat together the eggs, water, cayenne pepper, mustard, salt, and pepper.

Prepare the crispy coating: In a separate bowl combine the cornmeal, oats, herbs, salt, and pepper.

Dip the fillets in the egg wash, then dredge in the cornmeal mixture, pressing to coat well.

In a heavy 12-inch skillet heat the oil and butter over medium heat. When hot, place the fish fillets in the pan and cook about 4 minutes per side, or until golden. When the fillets are cooked, transfer to dinner plates. Top each fillet with 2 nickle-size slices of honey mustard butter. Place 2 lemon wedges on each plate and serve immediately.

PANFRIED CRISPY MACKEREL FILLETS

What makes these fillets crispy is a handsome coating of rolled oats. And the oats help off-set the natural oiliness of mackerel (it's the healthful Omega-3 oil here, so don't be concerned). The finishing touch is a piquant sauce. Make the sauce first to allow the flavors to develop while the mackerel is being prepared and cooked.

Mackerel is usually sold whole and is easy to fillet; see page 215 for details.

Serves 4

Sauce:

⅓ cup fresh lemon juice	*2 tablespoons Dijon mustard*
2 tablespoons fresh lime juice	*1 cup sour cream*
⅓ cup dry white wine	*1 tablespoon chopped fresh dill*
½ bay leaf	*1 tablespoon chopped fresh parsley*
1 tablespoon minced onion	*Salt and pepper to taste*

½ cup johnnycake meal	*2 cups rolled oats*
(white cornmeal)	*2 pounds mackerel fillets, skin removed*
Salt and pepper	*⅓ cup vegetable oil*
2 eggs, beaten	

To make the sauce:

✎   Place the lemon juice, lime juice, wine, bay leaf, and onion in a saucepan over medium heat. Bring to a low simmer and cook until the liquid is reduced by nearly half. In a bowl combine the mustard with the sour cream. Add the mixture to the saucepan, whisk, and return to a simmer. Continue cooking for an additional 2 minutes. Add the dill and parsley, stir, and remove from the heat. Season to taste with salt and pepper. Set aside.

To cook the fish:

✎   Set out 3 wide, shallow bowls: one for the cornmeal, seasoned with a little salt and pepper, one for the eggs, and one for the oats. Dip each fillet first in the cornmeal, then in the egg, and then in the rolled oats, pressing firmly in the oats to create a solid coating. Transfer each fillet to a platter until you have coated all the fillets.

✐ In a large, heavy 12-inch skillet heat the oil over medium heat. When hot but not smoking, gently place the fillets in the oil and cook for about 3 to 4 minutes on each side, or until golden. Turn carefully with a spatula. When the fish are done, transfer to a platter and serve immediately with the sauce on the side and plenty of lemon wedges.

OLD-FASHIONED FISH AND CHIPS

You can easily make great fish and chips at home even if you don't have a deep-fat fryer. I use a 10-inch cast-iron skillet with about half an inch of vegetable oil.

This is my idea of classic fish and chips: The fish is coated with a batter that becomes a crisp jacket floating around the tender juicy fish inside. We love this made with hake, but there are lots of other fish—sea trout, tilefish, haddock, or cod—that would do as well. Serve with tartar sauce and coleslaw.

Serves 4

Batter:

1 cup flour
1 teaspoon baking soda
Salt and pepper
3 eggs

6 tablespoons beer
3 tablespoons cider vinegar
3 tablespoons vegetable oil

For the chips:

2 pounds potatoes, peeled and cut into
*   french-fry sticks*
1½ cups vegetable oil for frying

For the fish:

> *2 pounds hake or haddock fillets or other firm fish*
> *Flour for dredging*

Note: If you are using a 10-inch skillet, you will need 1½ cups of vegetable oil to cook the fish and chips. If you are using a larger skillet, you will need slightly more to bring the oil to a depth of ½ inch.

To make the batter:
✂ In a large bowl sift together the flour, baking soda, and a pinch of salt and pepper. In a separate bowl beat the eggs. Add the beer, vinegar, and oil, and beat together well. Add to the dry ingredients and combine thoroughly. Set aside.

To make the chips:
✂ Soak the raw french-fry sticks in a bowl of cold water until you are ready to use them. Before frying, dry *thoroughly* with paper towels.
✂ Heat the oil in a 10-inch skillet over medium heat until it reaches 375 degrees. Add the potatoes, being careful not to splatter hot fat. Cook in batches for about 10 minutes, or until golden outside and tender inside. As the potatoes are cooked, transfer to a cookie sheet lined with brown paper. Sprinkle with salt and place in a warm oven with the heat turned off.

To cook the fish:
✂ Dredge each fillet in flour and then dip in the batter. Immediately place the coated fish carefully into the same hot oil in which you cooked the potatoes, still at a temperature of 375. Only coat as much fish as you can cook at one time; if you coat it all at once and set it on a platter, the batter will stick to the platter. Cook the fish until golden, about 1 minute or 2 per side. As the fish is done, transfer it with a slotted spatula to a cookie sheet lined with brown paper and place it in the oven with the fries. (While you are tending the cooking fish, use a slotted spoon to remove and discard any batter particles that float off the fish and begin to cook. They will burn, and if you leave them in the pan, they will flavor the oil with a burned taste.)
✂ As soon as all the fillets are cooked, serve them and the chips with tartar sauce, lots of lemon wedges, and a shaker bottle of cider vinegar.

SALT COD CAKES

Salt cod is an old-fashioned item, and in this recipe it is used very traditionally. But these fish cakes can be made with nearly any other fish as a substitute.

Because salt cod is preserved by salting, it must be soaked and rinsed a number of times over a twenty-four-hour period before it is used. Directions are on the wooden box that the fish comes in.

These make a very satisfying supper and are good served with Green Tomato Salsa (page 207) or a crisp green salad.

Makes 2 dozen

1 pound salt cod, soaked and rinsed	*2 eggs, beaten*
1 cup diced onion	*2 tablespoons softened butter*
3 tablespoons vegetable oil	*¼ cup freshly chopped parsley*
3 cups cooked mashed potatoes	*½ teaspoon freshly ground black pepper*
⅓ cup milk	

✍ Place the rinsed salt cod in a pan, add water to cover, and bring to a simmer over high heat. Lower the heat and cook at a simmer for 10 minutes.

✍ While the fish is cooking, gently cook the onion in 1 tablespoon of the vegetable oil in a skillet over medium heat. Cook until tender and translucent but not browned, then set aside.

✍ Drain the fish and flake it in a food processor or in a large bowl. Add the onion, mashed potatoes, milk, eggs, butter, parsley, and pepper, and mix thoroughly.

✍ Lightly flour your hands and form the fish/potato mixture into patties about 2½ inches to 3 inches in diameter and ½ inch thick. Heat the remaining 2 tablespoons of vegetable oil in a large skillet over medium heat. Cook the fish cakes until golden on both sides, turning once with a spatula, about 3 or 4 minutes per side. As the fish cakes are cooked, transfer to a plate in a warm oven until you have cooked them all. Serve hot.

COD PROVENÇALE

The beauty of this dish is its simplicity. Cod is pan-seared and then surrounded with a classic mix of "Provençale" vegetables—fresh plum tomatoes, onion, garlic, and black olives—to finish together in the pan.

Serves 4

2 tablespoons olive oil
2 tablespoons butter
⅔ cup chopped onion
1 clove garlic, minced
2 pounds cod fillets
8 plum tomatoes, peeled, seeded, and chopped

8 Kalamata olives or other brine-cured black olives, pitted and chopped
½ teaspoon chopped fresh thyme
1 tablespoon chopped fresh basil

✎ Place the oil and butter in a large, heavy skillet over medium heat. Add the onion and garlic, and cook, stirring occasionally, until the onion becomes tender and translucent but the garlic is not browned. Remove the vegetables from the pan, return the pan to the heat, and when it is hot but not smoking, add the cod fillets and allow to cook for about 1 minute.

✎ Return the onion and garlic to the pan with the fish. Add the tomatoes, olives, and thyme, sprinkling them over and around the fish. Turn the heat to medium-low, cover the skillet, and cook for about 3 to 4 minutes more, or until the fish is cooked thoroughly and the vegetables are tender and juicy.

✎ To serve, place a fillet on each plate and spoon the vegetables over the fish, using all the juices that form in the pan, too. Sprinkle some fresh basil over each and serve immediately.

COD WITH CIDER CREAM SAUCE

This combination of classic New England ingredients—cod, cider, and apples, served with johnnycakes—is a delicious and pretty main course. Pan-seared cod sits atop a johnnycake and is topped with caramelized apple slices and a cream sauce flavored with cider and fresh sage.

Serve extra johnnycakes on the side. Pureed butternut squash and braised brussels sprouts are excellent choices to complete the meal.

Both fish and chicken stock work well in the sauce.

Serves 4

2 tablespoons oil	½ cup cider vinegar
4 tablespoons butter	1½ teaspoons finely chopped
2 pounds cod, hake, or haddock fillets	fresh sage
2 Granny Smith apples, peeled, cored,	¼ cup fish or chicken stock
and cut in ¼-inch slices	1 cup light cream
¼ cup minced shallots	8 cooked johnnycakes (page 208)
½ cup apple cider	

❧ Heat the oil and 2 tablespoons of butter in a large, heavy skillet over medium heat. When hot but not smoking, place the fillets in the pan and cook until a crisp golden crust is formed on each side (the meat will be white, and cooked). Transfer to a platter, cover with a loose foil tent, and set in a warm oven with the heat turned off.

❧ Add the remaining 2 tablespoons of butter to the skillet and cook the apple slices over medium heat until tender and golden but not mushy. Transfer to a plate and set aside.

❧ Add the shallots to the skillet and cook until tender but not crisp. Add the cider and vinegar, and stir, scraping the bottom of the pan to loosen any bits. Add 1 teaspoon of the sage and bring to a simmer. Continue cooking and stirring until the liquid is reduced by nearly half. Add the stock, return to a simmer, and cook, stirring occasionally, until the liquid is reduced again by nearly half. Stir in the cream and gently place the cod in the sauce, trying to keep the fillets whole. Gently simmer for 1 minute (the mixture should be slightly thickened).

✍ Place 2 johnnycakes, slightly overlapping, on each plate. Using a slotted spatula, place a portion of cod on the johnnycakes. Arrange a few apple slices over the cod. Top with the sauce and sprinkle with the remaining ½ teaspoon of sage. (If you have any whole sage leaves left, arrange a few on the top of each serving.) Serve immediately.

Note: Cod tends to flake apart as it cooks, but don't let this worry you. Do your best to handle it gently and keep the fillets whole. As long as you don't push the cod around and turn it into hash, the flakes will be beautiful medallions on the plate.

SAUTÉED BLUEFISH WITH AN APPLE CRUST

Rich and flavorful bluefish is complemented by a crust of minced apple mixed with onion, fresh dill, and tangy Dijon mustard. Your dinner guests will be thrilled, and you'll be relaxed and happy because the assembled dish must sit for at least 6 hours, or overnight, before being pan-sautéed.

Credit for this absolutely delicious recipe goes to Normand Leclair, owner and chef of The Red Rooster Tavern in North Kingstown, Rhode Island.

Serves 4

*3 cups peeled and finely minced
  Granny Smith apples*
1 cup finely minced onion
½ cup chopped fresh dill
3 tablespoons Dijon mustard
3 tablespoons olive oil

*2 pounds bluefish fillets, with skin
  removed*
3 tablespoons butter
3 tablespoons white wine vinegar
Lemon wedges

✍ In a large bowl mix together the apples, onion, dill, mustard, and olive oil. Evenly pat a coating of this mixture on both sides of the fillets, using up all the mixture. Transfer the coated fillets to a large flat dish in a single layer. Cover and refrigerate for at least 6 hours.

✄ Melt the butter in a large, heavy skillet over medium heat. Carefully add the fillets without crowding and cook for about 3 to 5 minutes on the first side, or until a golden crust has formed. Carefully turn the fillets with a spatula so as not to disturb the crust, and cook the other side in the same manner.

✄ When all the fillets are cooked, transfer to plates or a serving platter.

✄ Keeping the skillet over medium heat, add the vinegar to the pan and stir, scraping any bits from the bottom of the pan. Cook for 30 seconds, then pour over the fish. Serve immediately with lemon wedges.

CURRIED MONKFISH

This dish has a beautiful golden sauce, full of warm curry flavors that lend themselves well to monkfish. Golden raisins add sweetness and a nice chewy texture. There is lots of sauce, so serve this over rice.

For a hotter curry, increase the curry powder.

Serves 6

2 tablespoons butter	1 cup golden raisins
¼ cup minced shallots	1 tablespoon curry powder
1 cup sliced mushrooms	3 egg yolks, beaten
1 cup Madeira wine	1½ cups milk or light cream
2½ pounds monkfish, cut in	
1-inch cubes	

✄ In a large (12-inch), heavy skillet melt the butter over medium heat. Add the shallots and mushrooms, and cook until tender but not browned. Add the Madeira and simmer over medium-low heat until the liquid is reduced by nearly half, about 5 minutes. Add the fish, raisins, and curry powder, and continue cooking for about 4 minutes; the fish is cooked when it turns white.

✄ In a large bowl beat the egg yolks with the milk or light cream. Add this to the skillet and stir the mixture gently over medium-low heat until it thickens sufficiently. This will take only a few minutes. Do *not* let the mixture boil. Serve immediately over rice.

MONKFISH STIR-FRY

This dish has a sauce with Asian flavors, lots of vegetables, and tender chunks of monkfish. It is quick to prepare, healthful, and delicious. Serve with rice.

This recipe is an adaptation of one from the collection of the Rhode Island Seafood Council.

Serves 4

4 tablespoons peanut oil	*2 cups quartered mushrooms*
2 cups sliced celery	*1 pound monkfish, cut in 1-inch cubes*
(cut at diagonal, ¼ inch thick)	*4 tablespoons flour*
1 cup sliced onion	*¼ cup soy sauce*
1 cup julienned red bell pepper	*2 tablespoons dry sherry*
3 cups finely sliced green cabbage	

✄ Heat 2 tablespoons of the oil in a wok or large chef's pan. When the oil is hot but not smoking, add the celery and stir-fry for a minute. Add the onion, stir, and cook for a minute. Add the red pepper, stir, and cook for a minute. Add the cabbage, stir, and cook for a minute. And lastly, add the mushrooms and continue cooking the mixture for about 2 minutes. Transfer to a platter.

✄ Add the remaining 2 tablespoons of oil to the wok (do not clean the wok). Dredge the cubed monkfish in the flour and add to the wok when the oil is hot but not smoking. Stir-fry for 3 to 4 minutes, or until the fish is white. Add the vegetables to the wok with the fish and toss. Combine the soy sauce with the sherry and pour into the wok. Toss the mixture until evenly coated. Remove from the heat and serve immediately over rice.

SZECHUAN TUNA

These spicy Asian flavors lend themselves very well to tuna. The fish is cooked along with broccoli and carrots; the brilliant colors of the vegetables make this an attractive dish. All you need to complete the meal is rice.

Shrimp also works very well in this recipe, in which case eggplant can be substituted for the broccoli and onions for the carrots.

The Chinese ingredients are easily found at any large supermarket or gourmet shop. Seeking them out is worth the effort.

Serves 4

2 cloves minced garlic	*1½ teaspoons cornstarch*
1 tablespoon minced fresh ginger	*1½ tablespoons water*
2 scallions, finely sliced on the diagonal	*1½ teaspoons sesame oil*
(Chinese cut)	*4 tablespoons vegetable oil*
3 tablespoons bean paste	*2 tablespoons chili pepper oil*
(also called bean sauce)	*4 cups broccoli florets*
1½ tablespoons dark soy sauce	*(about 2 pounds)*
3 tablespoons dry sherry	*1 cup julienned carrot*
3 tablespoons cider vinegar	*1 pound yellowfin tuna or any fresh*
3 tablespoons sugar	*tuna, cut in 1-inch chunks*
½ teaspoon Szechuan peppercorns	

➣ In a small bowl combine the garlic, ginger, and scallions. Set aside.

➣ In a glass measuring cup combine the bean paste, soy sauce, sherry, vinegar, and sugar. Crush the peppercorns with a mortar and pestle, and add to the bean paste mixture. Set aside.

➣ In a small glass dish combine the cornstarch with the water. Mix in the sesame oil and set aside.

➣ Place the vegetable oil and chili pepper oil in a large (12-inch), heavy skillet, chef's pan, or wok over medium-high heat. When the oil is hot but not smoking, add the garlic/ginger/

scallion mixture. Stir and cook for half a minute, until the mixture is fragrant but not browned. Add the broccoli and carrot. Continue cooking for 2 to 3 minutes more, stirring the mixture so that all ingredients are evenly coated with oil. Add the tuna and stir the ingredients so that the tuna becomes coated with the oil. Continue cooking for another 4 to 5 minutes, until the fish is cooked.

✺ Stir the bean paste mixture and pour into the pan. Stir quickly, coating all ingredients. Turn the heat to medium.

✺ Stir the cornstarch mixture and pour into the pan. Stir quickly to coat all ingredients. Keep on the heat for another minute. Toss and serve immediately over rice.

Tautog, a.k.a. Blackfish

Tautog, also known as blackfish, is a common fish in the rocky coastal waters of New England. It is easily caught from shore as well as from boats and is generally between 18 and 24 inches in length. The fillets are meaty, and one 6-pound fish will yield 3 pounds of fillets, easily feeding four to six people.

This fish has humanlike teeth and powerful jaws, and feeds on crabs, mussels, and clams—making it a very good source of calcium.

The carcass makes an excellent fish stock, so I suggest you buy tautog whole and fillet it at home.

STUFFED TAUTOG

Tautog is a meaty, flavorful fish, and its fillets lend themselves well to being split and stuffed—the fillets are thick and juicy and hold their shape as they bake. Here, the stuffing includes spinach and a few scallops, adding flavor and moisture. This dish can be assembled ahead and kept in the refrigerator until ready to bake, making it an easy but impressive dish for a dinner party.

When shopping for the fish, look for fillets that are about 1 inch thick or a whole fish of about 6 pounds, which will yield two large, meaty fillets of a pound and a half each. They can be cut in three sections each, yielding six pieces—perfect for this recipe.
Serves 6

Stuffing:

2 tablespoons butter
⅔ cup minced onion
1 cup minced celery
2 cloves garlic, pressed
1½ cups fresh bread crumbs
2 teaspoons finely chopped fresh parsley

⅔ cup packed fresh spinach,
cut into ribbons
1 tablespoon fresh lemon juice
1 tablespoon dry vermouth
¼ pound shucked scallops, chopped

3 pounds tautog fillets (6 thick fillets)
3 tablespoons butter
2 tablespoons fresh lemon juice
1 tablespoon dry vermouth

To make the stuffing:

☙ Heat the butter in a large, heavy skillet and add the onion, celery, and garlic. Cook, stirring, over medium heat until tender but not browned. Add the bread crumbs, stir, and continue cooking until they are golden. Transfer the mixture to a large bowl. Allow the mixture to cool slightly as you chop the parsley and cut the spinach. Add the parsley, spinach, lemon juice, and vermouth to the bread crumb mixture and toss. Add the scallops and blend thoroughly. Divide the stuffing into 6 equal portions.

⋖ Preheat oven to 350 degrees.

To stuff the fish:

⋖ Using a sharp fillet knife, butterfly each fillet; that is, split each fillet horizontally, leaving one end of the fillet intact so that the split produces a flap, not a new fillet—or make a "pocket" incision in the fillet. Place 1 portion of the stuffing in the opening and gently push the top of the fillet down over it.

⋖ Place the stuffed fillets in a baking pan. Top each with a half tablespoon of the butter and pour the lemon juice and vermouth over all. Cover the pan with foil and bake for 25 minutes, or until done. Serve immediately.

BROILED BLUEFISH WITH ANCHOVY VINAIGRETTE

The rich taste of bluefish is perfectly complemented by the bite of anchovy and vinegar.
Serves 4

2 pounds bluefish fillets	*2 teaspoons Dijon mustard*
¼ teaspoon freshly ground black pepper	*½ cup chopped fresh flat-leaf parsley*
¼ teaspoon salt	*3 teaspoons fresh lemon juice*
½ teaspoon grated lemon zest	*3 teaspoons white wine vinegar*
6 anchovy fillets	*6 tablespoons olive oil*

⋖ Preheat the broiler.

⋖ Place the fillets, skin side down, on a broiler pan lined with foil.

⋖ In a small bowl combine the pepper, salt, and lemon zest. Reserve ¼ teaspoon and use the rest to rub over the fillets.

✂ Place the remaining ingredients in a blender along with the reserved pepper/lemon zest mixture. Puree until the anchovies and parsley are finely minced.

✂ Place the fish under the broiler, no closer than 6 inches, and broil without turning for 12 to 15 minutes, until completely cooked.

✂ Remove the fish from the oven and transfer with a spatula to plates. Top with the anchovy sauce and serve immediately.

Hauling hands—a group of Block Island, Rhode Island, fishermen, 1920s.

Note the thick wool mittens these men are wearing. These were standard gear and were called "hauling hands." The mittens were knit oversize, with double-ply palms, then "boiled and beaten, beaten and boiled until they were tougher than felt; then they were worn among the muck and oil of fishing until they were virtually impermeable."

BROILED TILEFISH WITH RED PEPPER PESTO

Tilefish is so named for its colorful skin. Its meat is white, tender, and flavorful, and can be substituted for cod in many recipes. Here it is simply broiled and topped with a roasted red pepper "pesto," which can be made in advance and kept in the refrigerator until needed. Bring to room temperature before using.

   If you do not have a broiler, the fish can be sautéed.

Serves 4

2 red bell peppers, roasted
   (see page 209)
4 tablespoons grated Parmesan cheese
4 tablespoons olive oil

1 tablespoon chopped fresh
   flat-leaf parsley
1 tablespoon fresh lemon juice

2 pounds tilefish fillets
Salt and pepper

To make the red pepper pesto:

Skin and seed the roasted red peppers and finely chop. This should yield about 1 cup; reserve ¼ cup. Place all but the reserved pepper in a large bowl with the cheese, oil, parsley, and lemon juice. Mix together well and transfer to a food processor blender. Pulse until the mixture is slightly smoother but not completely pureed. Transfer to a mixing bowl and stir in the reserved ¼ cup of chopped pepper. Set aside.

To cook the fish:

Preheat the broiler.

Place the fillets in a broiler pan and sprinkle a little salt and pepper over each. Cook under the broiler, 6 inches from the heat source, until done, about 8 minutes. The meat will be white and piping hot.

Immediately transfer to plates and top each portion with a generous dollop of red pepper pesto. Serve immediately.

BROILED MACKEREL WITH MUSTARD BUTTER

The tangy mustard butter sauce is the perfect contrast to the rich taste of mackerel. It is also quick and easy to prepare. Make the mustard butter ahead of time.
Serves 4

MUSTARD BUTTER

> *1 tablespoon Dijon mustard*
> *2 tablespoons butter, softened*
> *2 tablespoons finely chopped*
>   *fresh parsley*
> *2 tablespoons fresh lemon juice*
>
> *2 pounds mackerel fillets*
> *1 tablespoon oil*
> *Salt and pepper*
> *½ tablespoon butter, cut in bits*
> *2 tablespoons fresh lemon juice*

To make the mustard butter:

✜➔ Mix all the mustard butter ingredients together well in a small bowl. Cover and refrigerate for at least 30 minutes.

To broil the mackerel:

✜➔ Preheat the broiler.

✜➔ Place the fillets, skin side down, in a broiler pan. Brush the tops with the oil and sprinkle with a little salt and pepper. Distribute the butter over the fillets. Place under the broiler, 6 inches from the heat source, and cook for 5 to 8 minutes, until done. Remove from the oven and immediately pour the lemon juice over the fillets. Transfer to plates.

✜➔ Top each serving with a generous teaspoon of the mustard butter and serve immediately.

ROASTED SALMON WITH CRISPY SKIN AND A CITRUS SAUCE

This is so simple and so delicious, you will turn to it again and again. The salmon is cooked on a bed of fresh herbs, skin side up, under the broiler, and when served, it is topped with a sauce of orange, lemon, and lime juices. If your fish market has only skinned salmon fillets, don't despair. The recipe still works: What had been the skin side becomes slightly crisp and sweet, almost caramelized.

Serves 4

2 pounds thick salmon fillets,
  not skinned
1 tablespoon olive oil
Salt and pepper to taste
1 bunch of fresh dill
  (to equal about 1 cup)

⅓ cup minced shallots
12 sprigs of fresh thyme about
  5 inches long
6 sprigs of fresh rosemary about
  5 inches long
½ cup dry vermouth

CITRUS SAUCE

Juice of 6 oranges (about 1½ cups)
Juice of 2 lemons (about ⅔ cup)
Juice of 2 limes (about ⅓ cup)

Preheat the broiler and position the rack 6 inches from the heat source.

To prepare the fish:

Rub the flesh side of the fillets with the olive oil and a little salt and pepper. In a lightly buttered 9-inch by 13-inch ovenproof glass baking dish, make an even layer of the dill (to just fit under the fillets and not beyond). Top the dill with the shallots, and top the shallots with the thyme and rosemary. Lay the fillets over the herbs, skin side up, and pour the vermouth over the fish.

➤ Place under the preheated broiler and cook until the skin is crisp and charred, 12 to 15 minutes. Combine the citrus juices in a saucepan over medium heat and cook at a simmer until reduced by half, about 10 minutes.

➤ Remove the fish from the oven and invert onto a platter. The herbs and shallots will stick to the fish; leave them there when you serve it. Top with the citrus sauce. Serve immediately.

FISH BAKED WITH PESTO

Pesto makes a great partner for baked fish, and you can use nearly any fish you like — striped bass, bluefish, hake, tilefish, cod, and haddock all work well.
Serves 4

2 pounds fish fillets	*1 tablespoon chopped fresh parsley*
¼ cup water	*¼ teaspoon paprika*
¼ cup dry white wine	*¾ cup thinly sliced onion*
¾ cup Basic Pesto (page 206)	*2 tablespoons fresh lemon juice*
½ cup fresh bread crumbs	*1 tablespoon butter, cut in bits*

➤ Preheat oven to 425 degrees.

➤ Place the fillets, skin side down, in a baking pan in a single layer. Add the water and wine to the baking pan. Spread the pesto evenly over the fillets.

➤ In a small bowl mix together the bread crumbs, parsley, and paprika. Sprinkle this mixture evenly over the pesto-topped fillets. Top the bread crumbs with the onion slices. Sprinkle the lemon juice over all and dot with butter.

➤ Place in the oven and bake for 20 minutes, or until the fish is completely cooked and piping hot. Serve immediately, pouring some of the cooking juices over each serving.

ROASTED WHOLE SEA BASS

Sea bass, when cooked, has the whitest meat I've ever seen. It literally gleams. It is also tender, juicy, and flavorful. It is an easy fish to fillet, but it is also a good candidate for baking whole. The meat lifts nicely off the bone, and the tender skin is edible or, if you prefer, easily pushed aside. The two things this technique has going for it are ease of preparation and the extra flavor gained by cooking on the bone.

Use this technique for roasting other whole fish, but for larger fish increase the liquid ingredients and the cooking time.

Serves 4

4 whole sea bass, about 1½ pounds each	*8 sprigs of fresh flat-leaf parsley*
Salt and pepper	*1 lemon, thinly sliced*
4 sprigs of fresh rosemary, about	*1 tablespoon olive oil*
4 inches long	*4 tablespoons fresh lemon juice*
8 sprigs of fresh thyme, about	*1 cup dry white wine*
4 inches long	*3 tablespoons butter, cut in bits*

> Preheat oven to 400 degrees.

> Trim any sharp fins from the fish. Scale, gut the fish, and remove the gills. Rinse quickly under cold running water. Rub the cavity of the fish with salt and pepper, and then stuff each with 1 sprig of rosemary, 2 sprigs of thyme, and 2 sprigs of parsley. Stuff 2 or 3 lemon slices, halved, into the cavities with the herbs. Rub the fish with olive oil and place in a lightly buttered baking pan. Pour the lemon juice and wine over the fish. Dot with the butter and place in the middle of the oven. Bake for 25 to 30 minutes, until the meat is white and completely cooked.

> Lift the fish out of the baking pan onto a platter and with a paring knife make an incision behind the head and at the tail. Then gently, with a small spatula, lift the fillet off the bones. Turn the fish over and repeat the process. Divide the fillets among the plates and pour the sauce from the baking pan over all. Serve immediately.

TUNA TERIYAKI

Use this recipe for tuna steaks or cubed tuna placed on skewers as kebabs. You can also substitute swordfish, tautog, monkfish, or shrimp for the tuna.
Serves 4 to 6

For the marinade:

½ cup soy sauce

½ cup dry sherry

2 tablespoons vegetable oil

4 tablespoons finely minced fresh
   gingerroot

2 teaspoons sugar

2 cloves garlic, pressed

2 pounds tuna steaks

✂ Combine all the marinade ingredients in a bowl and whisk together well. Place the tuna in a single layer in a glass baking pan. Pour the marinade over the tuna, cover, and refrigerate for at least 1 hour, turning and basting the meat halfway through.

✂ To cook, place steaks in a lightly oiled grill pan or on a grilling rack set about 8 inches above the hot coals of an outdoor grill. Cook for about 5 minutes per side. When done, the meat will flake apart. Serve immediately.

MONKFISH KEBABS

Monkfish meat is very firm and easily cubed, making it an excellent fish for the grill. Be sure to remove the skin; it is inedible.

This recipes requires that the fish and vegetables marinate for at least 2 hours before grilling.

Serves 6

Marinade:

1½ cups olive oil
1½ cups vegetable oil
¾ cup red wine vinegar
¼ cup fresh lemon juice
1 tablespoon Worcestershire sauce

3 cloves fresh garlic, crushed
1 tablespoon chopped fresh basil
1 tablespoon chopped fresh parsley
1 teaspoon chopped fresh dill
Salt and pepper to taste

4 medium-size onions, cut in quarters
3 bell peppers, cut in chunks
18 large mushrooms
18 cherry tomatoes

2 small zucchini, cut in
½-inch-thick slices
2 pounds monkfish, cut in generous
1-inch cubes

Whisk all the marinade ingredients together. Place the cubed monkfish in a large bowl and ladle approximately 1 cup of marinade over the fish. Gently toss the fish to coat, cover the bowl with plastic wrap, and refrigerate.

Place the vegetables in a large bowl and cover with the marinade. Toss gently. Cover with plastic wrap and refrigerate. (If you find the vegetables have more than sufficient marinade, add the extra to the fish.)

To cook:

Arrange the vegetables evenly on skewers, using some of each on every skewer. Place the monkfish on separate skewers. Place the kebabs on a hot grill and cook, turning frequently, for about 15 minutes. The fish should be opaque throughout, but be careful not to overcook.

✠ Serve immediately with rice or potatoes.

Sighting a range, ca. 1900.

Navigation skills are crucial to fishermen. Grandfathers and even fathers of today's generation of New England fishermen used ranges to orient themselves on their way to fishing grounds and on their way back home. To calculate a set of ranges a fisherman makes a notation of two sets of things that line up on shore from where he is on the water, using the points of the compass for reference. Becoming accomplished at this took time.

Phil Schwind, a Cape Cod fisherman, recounts an experience with a young man learning to figure ranges: "You see that white spot on top of Dr. Hill's rock? Well, that white spot lines up with that brown rock in the middle of the field." Yes, Phil said, "except that white spot is a seagull which is apt to fly away anytime, and the brown rock you ranged on is a cow—and she's already moved."

MONKFISH FAJITAS

Fajitas have become an American favorite, adapted in all kinds of ways from their Mexican origins. Here, chunks of marinated and grilled monkfish are layered along with fresh tomato, avocado, onion, lettuce, cheese, and salsa, and wrapped in a soft flour tortilla. Delicious, and a fun meal-in-one-dish. Shrimp or swordfish can be substituted for the monkfish. *Serves 4 (2 fajitas per person)*

Marinade:

½ cup olive oil

¼ cup fresh lime juice

2 teaspoons fresh lemon juice

2 tablespoons finely chopped
fresh cilantro

1 clove garlic, pressed

1 jalapeño pepper, finely minced

Salt and pepper

1 pound monkfish, cut in 1-inch cubes

For the fajitas:

2 ripe avocados, peeled, pits removed,
and chopped

2 cups diced tomatoes

2 cups shredded lettuce

1 cup chopped red onion

1 tablespoon finely chopped fresh
cilantro

1 teaspoon fresh lime juice

Salt and pepper

½ cup sour cream

8 large, soft flour tortillas

½ cup grated Monterey Jack cheese

1 cup salsa (as hot as you like)

To marinate the fish:

Combine all the marinade ingredients in a large bowl. Add the chunks of monkfish and toss well. Cover and refrigerate for at least 1 hour.

To cook the fish:

⮡ Cook the marinated fish in a lightly oiled and hot grill pan over medium heat, turning, until the fish is golden and completely cooked. Transfer to a platter.

To make the fajitas:

⮡ In a large bowl combine the avocado, tomatoes, lettuce, onion, cilantro, and lime juice. Toss and season to taste with salt and pepper.

⮡ Spread a little sour cream down the center of each tortilla in a 1-inch-wide strip. Over that place a portion of the vegetable mixture. Top that with some monkfish, a little grated cheese, and a tablespoon of salsa. Roll the tortilla around the filling. Place 2 on each plate and serve immediately, with more salsa on the side.

Superstitions

Fishermen hold to a number of superstitions not familiar to the rest of us. Here are some of the more common ones:

Don't turn a hatch cover upside down.

Don't whistle, it whistles up a breeze.

Don't mention "pig" on board.

Don't shave on a trip.

Don't leave for a trip on a Friday.

Don't return a knife in any way other than it was given.

Don't put your hat in your bunk.

Thirteen-pot trawls are bad luck.

Don't leave the dock twice in the same day.

Don't take women on a trip.

Don't brag, it brings bad luck.

Don't serve beef stew aboard; it brings on a gale.

SMOKED HADDOCK CASSOULET

We were experimenting with some smoked haddock when I thought it might be interesting to use it in a cassoulet dish in place of the traditional meat. The results are a hearty casserole chock-full of cold-weather vegetables and the traditional white beans, all flavored with the smoky old-time taste of finnan haddie. This healthful meal is perfect for the middle of winter and is one of those dishes that is even better the next day.

If the finnan haddie is very salty, soak it for an hour or so in a couple of changes of fresh warm water. Rinse and pat dry.

Serves 6 to 8

1 cup dried navy beans, sorted, washed, and soaked overnight	*6 peppercorns*
1 small Savoy cabbage (1 pound)	*1 teaspoon chopped fresh thyme*
4 slices bacon, diced	*1½ cups water*
1½ cups sliced leeks (¼-inch slices)	*½ cup dry white wine*
1 cup coarsely chopped onion	*2 cups diced potatoes*
3½ cups julienned turnips	*2 pounds finnan haddie, cut in 3-inch chunks*
1½ cups julienned carrots	*1 cup fresh bread crumbs*
1 tablespoon minced garlic	*2 tablespoons butter, cut in bits*

Drain the beans and place in a saucepan with enough water to cover. Place over high heat and bring to a boil. Lower the heat, cover the pot, and cook at a simmer for 1 hour, or until the beans are tender but not mushy. Drain and set aside.

Core and quarter the cabbage. Bring a large pot of lightly salted water to a boil. Drop in the cabbage and cook, uncovered, for 5 minutes. Drain in a colander and set aside.

Place the bacon in a large, heavy skillet over medium heat. Cook until the bacon has rendered its fat but has not become crisp, then remove with a slotted spoon and set aside. Add the leeks, onion, turnips, carrots, and garlic to the hot bacon fat and cook over medium heat, stirring occasionally, until the garlic is fragrant but not browned. Remove from the heat.

Combine the navy beans, sautéed vegetables, bacon, peppercorns, and thyme in a Dutch oven. Add the water and wine, place over medium heat, and bring to a simmer. Cook at a low simmer, partially covered, for about 1 hour. (Lift the lid and stir the mixture occasionally.) After an hour most but not all of the liquid should be gone. Add the potatoes in a single layer, then the cabbage, then the fish. Cover and cook at a simmer for an additional 30 minutes.

Preheat oven to 350 degrees.

Gently stir the cassoulet to combine the ingredients. Transfer to a wide, shallow casserole dish, top with the bread crumbs, and distribute the bits of butter over the bread crumbs. Place in the oven for 20 minutes. Serve hot, with sourdough bread and sweet butter.

Underutilized Species

There are over two thousand species of finfish in the coastal waters of the United States and Canada, and of this number, only about five hundred are actually harvested for human food. Out of the five hundred, there really are only about a dozen species that are generally accepted by the American consumer.

7

Main Course — Shellfish

A New England lobsterman with a good one, 1970s.

Lobster fishing in New England is still done mostly with small boats and a crew of two, leaving early in the morning (weather permitting) and returning at the end of the same day.

Basic Steamed Shellfish:

1. Lobster
2. Crabs
3. Shrimp
4. Clams or Mussels

Basic Sautéed Shellfish

Basic Grilled or Broiled Shellfish Kebabs

Basic Grilled or Broiled Shellfish in the Shell

Mussels Steamed in Wine and Herbs

Spicy Cajun Shrimp

Stuffed Squid

Crab Cakes

Oyster Bread Pudding

Lobster Pie

Crab Soufflé

How to Select and Store Live Lobsters and Shellfish

Lobster Facts

The shellfish harvested in the waters off New England are some of the best in the world. Our lobsters are considered a delicacy in places as far away as Norway and Japan. Many people visiting coastal New England look forward to a simple steamed lobster dinner as much as they look forward to any other part of their trip.

The recipes in this section will tell you how to make the most of this bounty. First, you will find directions for the simplest treatment of all—steaming (the easiest and quickest way to prepare fresh shellfish), followed by directions for sautéeing, baking, and grilling, all done quite plainly but the perfect choice if you are in a hurry, or if you want a simple meal of unadulterated seafood tastes. Beyond that, you'll find plenty of ideas for "doing" something with lobster, crab, shrimp, squid, oysters, mussels, and clams.

Don't dismiss shellfish as too expensive for everyday dining. Live rock crabs, mussels, and clams are a real bargain and very versatile, as these recipes will show you. Lump crabmeat is more than ten times the cost of live crabs because picking the meat from rock crabs is a bit of a chore, but if everybody pitches in, the job is over in no time.

BASIC STEAMED SHELLFISH

For many people this is the absolute best way to eat shellfish. It is also exceedingly simple.

The steps for steaming lobster, crab, shrimp, clams, or mussels are virtually the same. The cooking time varies, and the cooking liquid can be seasoned. Clams and mussels must be scrubbed well with a stiff brush under cold running water before cooking, and mussels must be debearded.

You need a very large pot with a lid to steam shellfish (I use one 14 inches in diameter by 11 inches tall). For shrimp, clams, or mussels it is helpful but not necessary to have a pot with a set-in, removable strainer.

The cooking liquid from clams and mussels makes excellent fish stock for soups and sauces. You can save the liquid from shrimp if it is not too highly seasoned.

Basic Steps:

1. Put cold water (or other cooking liquid) in the pot to a depth of 2 inches. Add seasonings if using.
2. Bring the water to a boil over high heat.
3. When the water reaches a boil, add the shellfish and cover the pot tightly. Note: The pot can be crowded, but do not try to layer lobsters or crabs more than three deep. Instead, use two pots.
4. When the water returns to a boil, set the timer.
5. When the cooking time is complete, remove the pot from the heat, then remove the shellfish from the pot. Use tongs for lobsters and crabs, and a slotted spoon for shrimp, clams, and mussels (unless you have a pot with a removable strainer). Set lobsters and crabs in a colander to drain and cool for 1 or 2 minutes before serving. Serve shrimp, clams, and mussels immediately.
6. To save the broth from clams or mussels for fish stock: Place the uncovered pot over high heat, bring to a boil, and simmer for 5 minutes. When cool, pour the broth through a fine-mesh sieve lined with a double layer of dampened cheesecloth into a glass container with a lid. Refrigerate until ready to use. Otherwise, place in a freezer container and store in freezer until ready to use.

SHELLFISH	COOKING TIME
Lobsters of 1½ pounds each Cooking Liquid: *Water*	12 minutes
Rock Crabs of 1 pound each Cooking Liquid: *Water* 　　　*½ cup vinegar and/or beer* 　　　*1 bay leaf* 　　　*¼ teaspoon whole black peppercorns* 　　　*2 tablespoons hot red pepper flakes*	10 minutes
Shrimp, medium Cooking Liquid: *Water* 　　　*2 tablespoons fresh lemon juice* 　　　*½ teaspoon cayenne pepper* 　　　*¼ teaspoon dry mustard* 　　　*1 bunch celery leaves*	5 minutes
Clams or Mussels Cooking Liquid: *Equal parts water and dry white wine*	5 minutes

Serving Tips:

✎ At each place setting have a bowl of lemon wedges and a bowl of melted butter or cocktail sauce or strained broth. And for lobster or crab you'll need to provide tools (nut crackers and crab forks). Lots of napkins are necessary (some people like bibs) because eating steamed shellfish is a messy affair. Set a large bowl in the center of the table for the empty shells.

✎ Lobster, crab, and shrimp are also good served cold, with lemon wedges, cocktail sauce, or homemade Herbed Mayonnaise (page 204).

Lobster: After the cooked lobsters have cooled for a minute or two, split them down the stomach and tail with a sharp knife and crack the claws in a couple of places before serving.

Crab: After the cooked crabs have cooled for a minute or two, set them on a board and give them a rap with a kitchen mallet in a couple of places before you serve them.

Clams or mussels: When the cooking time is complete, use a slotted spoon or tongs to remove the ones that have opened (this should be most of them) and place in a colander set over a bowl. Cover the pot again and allow the unopened clams or mussels to cook for another minute or two. Discard any that do not open.

BASIC SAUTÉED SHELLFISH

This is handy when you just want to do something quick and simple with scallops or shrimp.
Serves 4

> *1 tablespoon olive oil*
> *1 tablespoon butter*
> *1¼ pounds shucked scallops*
>   *(or peeled and deveined shrimp)*

Heat the oil and butter in a large, heavy skillet over medium heat. When the butter is sizzling, add the scallops without crowding the pan. After about a minute, use a metal spatula to loosen a scallop (the first crust they form will stick to the pan) and turn it with tongs. If it has developed a nice golden crust, you can turn all the scallops. Continue cooking and turning the scallops until they have a nice golden crust on all sides, 4 to 6 minutes. Serve immediately, with lemon wedges.

Note: Shrimp will cook a little faster than scallops and will not develop as much of a crust, but they should have some golden edges.

Handlining out of Southwest Harbor, Maine, 1940s.

Setting a long line with baited hooks at numerous intervals is an old method of fishing still in use today.

Like many Maine fishermen, this one was probably also engaged in other fisheries at different times of the year—including lobstering, shrimping, and fish trapping.

Clam Sizes

Fresh clams sold in the shell are divided into four size categories: littleneck (the smallest), topneck, cherrystone, and quahog (the largest). The smaller the clam, the more tender the meat.

Steamers are thin-shelled clams, generally a uniform size comparable to littleneck clams. They are never served raw but instead are steamed and served with their strained broth and melted butter.

BASIC GRILLED OR BROILED SHELLFISH KEBABS

Shucked scallops and oysters, and peeled and deveined shrimp, can be skewered and cooked on a hot grill over an outdoor fire or under a broiler.

Marinating for an hour or two is the best way to prepare shellfish for the grill, but you can skip that step if you're in a big hurry.

Serves 4

> *1¼ pounds shucked scallops or oysters*
>   *or cleaned shrimp*
> *Bamboo skewers soaked for 15 minutes*
>   *in cold water*
> *Marinade (see page 132) or 2*
>   *tablespoons olive oil*

⚒ Thread the scallops or oysters or shrimp on the skewers, barely touching. Brush them with marinade or olive oil. Place on a clean, lightly oiled grilling rack set about 8 inches above the hot coals or under a broiler. Cook, turning, until all sides are golden. Serve with lemon wedges.

Note: Because oysters are so soft, it is usually best when cooking them on skewers to wrap them with a piece of partially cooked bacon or to sandwich them between chunks of vegetables.

BASIC GRILLED OR BROILED SHELLFISH IN THE SHELL

Clams and oysters in the shell can be broiled or grilled, and as they cook their shells open. They can be served hot or chilled, with lemon wedges or cocktail sauce, or with Herbed Mayonnaise (page 204).

Live crabs and lobsters can also be cooked on a grill over a hot fire, but I have never found that method very satisfactory.

Makes 24

> *12 oysters in the shell*
> *12 littleneck clams in the shell*
> *2 tablespoons melted butter*
> *2 tablespoons fresh lemon juice*

To broil:

⚒ Scrub the oysters and clams well with a stiff brush under cold running water. Place side by side on a cookie sheet and place under a hot broiler about 6 inches from the heat source. Cook until the shells begin to open, 4 to 6 minutes. Remove from the oven, and when cool enough to handle, remove and discard the top shells. Dribble a little melted butter and lemon juice over each and return to the oven to broil for an additional 1 to 2 minutes, or until the juice in the shells is bubbling.

To grill:

✂ Set the oysters and clams on the grilling rack about 6 inches above the heat source. Cover with a lid or foil. After about 4 minutes, lift the lid and check to see if the top shells have opened. Follow the directions above.

Note: Place the oysters flat side up for either cooking method. Then you will have the deeper shell left to hold the oyster and juices.

MUSSELS STEAMED IN WINE AND HERBS

This is my version of Moules Marinière, that marvelous and simple French dish. The mussels are served in their handsome blue-black shells along with a fragrant broth. Serve this with hunks of a good crusty bread to soak up the juices at the bottom of the soup bowl. *Serves 4*

6 pounds live mussels
  (shells of about 2 to 2½ inches)
2 cups dry white wine
1 large clove garlic, minced
¼ cup minced shallot

½ teaspoon chopped fresh thyme
1 bay leaf
2 tablespoons butter, cut in bits
⅓ cup chopped fresh parsley

✂ Clean the mussels by scrubbing them well under cold running water and debeard.
✂ Place the wine, garlic, shallot, thyme, and bay leaf in a large stockpot. Bring to a boil, lower the heat, and simmer for 10 minutes. Add the mussels, cover the pot, and raise the

heat to high. Cook for 3 to 5 minutes, until all the shells have opened. (Discard any that do not open.)

⚮ With a slotted spoon transfer the mussels to 4 good-size soup bowls. After the last mussel is out of the pot, raise the heat, add the butter, and stir (it will melt almost immediately). When the butter has melted, remove the pot from the heat, stir in the parsley, and ladle over the mussels in the soup plates, using all the broth. Serve immediately.

SPICY CAJUN SHRIMP

A mix of spices and beer make a dark, thick sauce around the shrimp—very flavorful and perfect over rice.
Serves 4

2 teaspoons cayenne pepper
1 teaspoon black pepper
1 teaspoon crushed red pepper
½ teaspoon salt
1 teaspoon dried thyme
2 teaspoons dried basil
1 teaspoon dried oregano
⅔ cup butter

3 cloves garlic, minced
2 teaspoons Worcestershire sauce
2 cups diced tomato
2 pounds medium shrimp, peeled and
* deveined*
½ cup beer, at room temperature
4 cups hot cooked rice

⚮ In a small bowl combine the 3 peppers, salt, thyme, basil, and oregano.

⚮ Place the butter in a large (12-inch) skillet over medium heat. Add the spice mixture, garlic, and Worcestershire sauce, and stir. When the butter is melted, add the tomato. Place the shrimp over the tomatoes and cook, stirring occasionally, for about 2 minutes. Pour in the beer, cover, and cook at a simmer for another minute, or until the shrimp are pink with golden edges. Remove from the heat.

To serve:

⤞ Place some rice on each plate and top with a portion of shrimp and sauce. Serve immediately.

STUFFED SQUID

Here is an elegant way to serve squid. The bodies are filled with a savory stuffing, lightly sautéed, and topped with a simple wine sauce. The stuffing can be prepared in advance, and the squid can be stuffed and kept in the refrigerator until you are ready to finish the dish. *Serves 4*

½ cup olive oil	*3 cloves garlic, minced*
8 large squid, cleaned and tentacles	*2 cups fresh bread crumbs*
chopped (see page 25)	*¼ cup chopped fresh flat-leaf parsley*
¼ cup finely chopped onion	*Salt and pepper to taste*
¼ cup finely chopped celery	*2 cups dry white wine*
½ cup finely chopped mushrooms	

⤞ Place ¼ cup of the olive oil in a large, heavy skillet over medium heat. When it is hot, add the chopped squid tentacles, onion, celery, mushrooms, and garlic, cooking until tender and fragrant but not browned. Add the bread crumbs and stir until all ingredients are well combined and the bread crumbs are golden. Season to taste with salt and pepper. Remove from the heat and transfer the mixture to a large bowl. Stir in the parsley and set aside.

⤞ When the bread crumb mixture has cooled, stuff each squid about three-quarters full (the stuffing will expand when cooked). Close the end with a toothpick. If there is any leftover stuffing, you can put some on each plate when you serve the squid.

⤞ When all the squid are stuffed, divide the remaining ¼ cup of olive oil between 2 large skillets and place over medium heat. When the oil is hot, add the stuffed squid bodies and cook, turning, for 1 or 2 minutes, until the squid is turning white and has golden edges. Add

1 cup of wine to each pan, lower the heat, and cover. Cook for about 8 minutes more, occasionally basting and turning the squid. Remove the squid from the pans and transfer to serving plates—2 stuffed squid per person. Leave the wine mixture uncovered in the warm pans while you cut each squid on the diagonal into three sections. Remove the toothpicks. Pour some warm wine sauce over each serving and serve immediately.

CRAB CAKES

Crab cakes make a wonderful main course for lunch or dinner. Serve them with a green salad or coleslaw and, if you like, a dollop of Herbed Tartar Sauce (page 206).

For a memorable Sunday brunch, make eggs Benedict using crab cakes instead of Canadian bacon: Place the poached eggs on the hot crab cakes and top with Blender Hollandaise sauce (page 205).

Makes eighteen 3-inch cakes

2 pounds fresh lump crabmeat	3 tablespoons melted butter, cooled
¼ cup finely chopped fresh parsley	⅓ cup milk
¼ cup minced onion	1 teaspoon Worcestershire sauce
½ cup minced celery	2 tablespoons fresh lemon juice
¼ cup minced green bell pepper	½ teaspoon paprika
1 cup corn kernels	¼ teaspoon cayenne pepper
(fresh or frozen, thawed)	¼ teaspoon salt
1 clove garlic, pressed	½ cup cornmeal
2 cups fresh bread crumbs	Vegetable oil
3 eggs, beaten	

Pick over the crabmeat for shells and place in a large bowl. Add the parsley, onion, celery, bell pepper, corn, and garlic, and mix together. Add the bread crumbs and toss to distribute evenly.

✎ In a separate bowl whisk together the eggs, butter, milk, Worcestershire sauce, lemon juice, paprika, cayenne pepper, and salt.

✎ Add the egg mixture to the crab mixture and combine thoroughly. Form into 3-inch cakes, sprinkle each side with cornmeal, and transfer to a cookie sheet. (If the mixture is not moist enough to form cakes, add a little milk.) Cover with plastic wrap and refrigerate for at least 1 hour.

✎ When ready to cook, pour vegetable oil into a large, heavy skillet to a depth of ¼ inch. Heat the oil over medium heat, and when it is hot, add the crab cakes and cook them until golden on both sides (about 4 minutes per side). You will probably have to cook the crab cakes in batches; as they are done, transfer to a platter in a warm oven. Serve hot.

OYSTER BREAD PUDDING

This is a creamy, chock-full-of-oysters bread pudding, enhanced by onions and red peppers caramelized in rendered bacon fat—midwinter comfort food at its best. Add a romaine lettuce salad and some wine, and settle in for the evening.

This recipe is an adaptation of a favorite from the Gatehouse Restaurant in Providence, Rhode Island.

Serves 4 to 6

2 strips bacon	*½ teaspoon chopped fresh marjoram*
1 tablespoon olive oil	*Pinch of salt and pepper*
1 cup thinly sliced onion rings	*5 eggs*
⅔ cup finely diced red bell pepper	*2¼ cups shucked oysters, coarsely*
1 cup sliced mushrooms	*chopped (with ½ cup liquid reserved*
2⅔ cups milk	*for this recipe)*
1 cup light cream	*5 cups bread cubes from top-quality*
2 bay leaves	*French or Italian bread*
½ teaspoon chopped fresh thyme	*(cut roughly ½ inch to 1 inch)*

⧓ Preheat oven to 350 degrees.

⧓ In a large, heavy skillet cook the bacon until it is crisp and has rendered its fat. Remove the bacon and transfer it to brown paper to drain; when it has cooled, crumble and set aside. Add the olive oil to the bacon fat and place over medium heat. When hot, add the onion, stir once, and turn the heat to low. Cover and cook for 10 minutes, occasionally removing the cover to stir. Add the red pepper and mushrooms, and continue cooking over low heat, covered, occasionally removing the cover to stir, for an additional 10 minutes.

Oysterman in skiff, Connecticut, 1940s.

At the turn of the century southern New England's oyster beds were as famous as those of the Chesapeake. Hurricanes, the Great Depression, disputes over use-rights, and pollution all contributed to their decline. A renewed interest in oyster farming, cleaner waters, and consumer demand for this delicacy are bringing oyster beds back.

>н In a heavy saucepan combine the milk, cream, bay leaves, thyme, marjoram, salt, and pepper. Scald over medium heat, then set aside to cool.

>н In a large bowl beat the eggs well. When the scalded milk has cooled, remove and discard the bay leaves and add the milk to the eggs, whisking well. Add the oysters, ½ cup of their liquid, bread cubes, and caramelized vegetables. Mix gently but thoroughly with a spoon, cover, and refrigerate for 30 minutes.

>н Pour the mixture into a buttered 2-quart soufflé dish. Set the dish in a wide baking pan with an inch or two of water in it (enough to extend halfway up the sides of the soufflé dish). Bake for 50 to 60 minutes, until the top is golden and the pudding has begun to pull away from the sides of the dish. Remove to a cooling rack, let sit for 3 minutes, and serve.

Note: For an elegant first course, bake the puddings in individual buttered custard cups. (This recipe would fill twelve, so for a party of six, halve the recipe.) Reduce the baking time by about 10 minutes.

How to Select and Store Live Lobsters and Shellfish

Look for lively lobsters—ones that are actively moving about in the tank. Soft-shelled lobsters are just as tasty as hard-shelled lobsters; the shell is soft because it's new.

Transport your lobsters home in a sturdy bag or empty cooler, covered with a layer of newspaper, and put them in the crisper drawer of your refrigerator. Do not store them in water or crushed ice! They will keep in a crisper drawer for a day or so. The cool temperature puts them in an almost dormant state, but when you remove them from the refrigerator, they should start to move around. Never cook crabs or lobsters that have died! Instead, bury them deep in your garden or compost pile.

LOBSTER PIE

This is a simple, old-fashioned treat with a single flaky pastry crust on the bottom, a filling of chunks of lobster nestled in a creamy cheddar sauce, and a top crust of fresh herbed bread crumbs.

When my husband was a lobsterman, from 1985 to 1992, I had many occasions to find uses for leftover lobster. This is one of the recipes I developed.

Makes one 9-inch deep-dish pie

Filling:

2 tablespoons butter
2 tablespoons minced shallots
1 clove garlic, pressed
2 tablespoons unbleached flour
1¼ cups milk

¼ cup dry white wine or vermouth
Salt and pepper to taste
1½ cups grated cheddar cheese
1 pound cooked lobster meat,
    coarsely chopped

Topping:

2 tablespoons butter
1 cup fresh bread crumbs
1 teaspoon chopped fresh parsley

½ teaspoon chopped fresh thyme
1 clove garlic, pressed
Pinch of salt and pepper

1 Basic Piecrust (page 202)

To make the filling:

In a large, heavy skillet melt the butter over medium heat. Add the shallots and garlic, and cook until tender and fragrant but not browned. Sprinkle with the flour and stir until the flour is incorporated in the butter. Slowly whisk in the milk, allowing the mixture to thicken slightly each time before adding more. After all the milk has been added and the

Draggerman has his picture taken with an old and lucky lobster
(they continue to increase in size as they age) before throwing him back, 1990s.

sauce is fairly thick, add the wine and continue stirring and cooking until the mixture thickens again. Add the grated cheese and stir gently until the cheese melts. Remove from the heat and add the lobster meat. Set aside.

To make the bread crumb topping:

✄ Melt the butter in a large skillet over medium heat. Add the bread crumbs, parsley, thyme, garlic, salt, and pepper, and toss lightly until the bread crumbs are golden. Remove from the heat and set aside.

✄ Preheat the oven to 350 degrees.

To assemble the pie:

Roll out the piecrust to about an ⅛ inch thickness and drape over a 9½-inch-diameter deep-dish pie plate. Trim the dough to a half-inch overhang, turn the extra dough under, and crimp the edge. Pour in the lobster filling and top with an even layer of the herbed bread crumbs. (At this point it may look as if you should have used a regular pie plate, but you need the deep-dish plate so the filling won't bubble up over the edges as it bakes.)

⊱ Bake for 45 minutes, or until the pastry is golden and the top is bubbling. Remove from the oven, transfer to a rack, and let sit for a few minutes before cutting into wedges to serve.

Lobster Facts

- A lobster is the size of a mosquito when it is born.
- A lobster is approximately seven years old before it weighs a pound and is legal to keep.
- As a lobster grows, it sheds its shell, increasing in weight by 25 percent each time. It will go through this process, known as molting, twenty to thirty times before it reaches 1 pound.
- A lobster's age is approximately its weight multiplied by four plus three years.
- Lobsters eat fish, other crustaceans, and mollusks.
- Lobsters live on the ocean floor and store food by burying it; they will defend the food stash much as a dog does.
- A one-clawed lobster is called a cull and is less expensive than a lobster with both claws intact.

CRAB SOUFFLÉ

This is creamy and light inside, with a delicate crust on top and a wonderful crab and tarragon flavor throughout.

Soufflés are not as hard to make as you may think. You do need a soufflé dish, because the straight sides are important to the proper rising, and you can't have people running through the kitchen slamming doors, jumping up and down, or otherwise creating a ruckus. This will cause the soufflé to "fall" while it's still in the oven.

A soufflé will collapse slightly when you serve it, but don't let this concern you. Be sure to have everything else you're serving with the soufflé ready to go, though, before you take it out of the oven. The sooner you serve it, the better.

Makes one 9-inch soufflé (2-quart soufflé dish)

Butter to grease soufflé dish
3 tablespoons grated Parmesan cheese
4 tablespoons butter
3 tablespoons minced scallions
4½ tablespoons flour
1½ cups milk
6 eggs, divided, plus an additional
    egg white

⅔ cup grated Fontina cheese
4 teaspoons fresh lemon juice
1½ teaspoons Dijon mustard
Salt and pepper to taste
1 cup cooked crabmeat (about ½ pound)
2 tablespoons finely chopped fresh
    tarragon
¼ teaspoon cream of tartar

Thoroughly butter the soufflé dish and sprinkle in the Parmesan cheese, tilting the dish so that it is evenly coated.

Preheat oven to 400 degrees.

Melt the butter in a large saucepan over medium heat. Add the scallions and cook until tender but not browned. Sprinkle in the flour and stir until it is incorporated with the butter. Gradually add the milk, stirring constantly, and allow the mixture to thicken each time before adding more milk. When all the milk has been added and the mixture is thick, remove from the heat and whisk in the egg yolks, one at a time. Add the cheese, lemon juice, mustard, salt, and pepper, stirring well. Add the crabmeat and tarragon, and mix until completely blended. Transfer to a large bowl.

✎ In a large, deep glass bowl beat the egg whites until foamy. Add the cream of tartar and continue beating until they are stiff but not dry.

✎ Gently fold the beaten egg whites into the crab mixture (not the other way around) but do not beat them in — fold gently. The little clusters of stiff egg white are what will make the soufflé rise properly. Pour into the prepared soufflé dish. In the indentation at the top of the dish, run your thumb around the edge of the soufflé, creating a little groove.

✎ Place in the middle of the oven, lower the heat to 375 degrees, and bake for about 40 minutes, until the top of the soufflé is puffy and golden and the sides are coming away from the dish. Serve immediately.

How to Store Seafood

Fresh filleted or shucked seafood should be refrigerated in covered glass containers until you are ready to cook it. For some reason fish stays fresher longer when sitting in glass rather than plastic. This is particularly noticeable with certain seafood, such as scallops, which will quickly become slimy and develop a bad odor when stored in a plastic bag or container. Stored in glass, however, scallops stay sweet and fresh for days.

8

Vegetables

Fishing schooner captain at the helm, 1918.

"The world is not crowded with men eager to go winter bank fishing. . . . Wrestling with the vast sea breeds real humility, but it also breeds self-reliance and self-respect—that man has got something that isn't deserting him in a hurry."

—James B. Connolly, *The Book of Gloucester Fishermen*

Potatoes Anna

Corn Pudding

Spinach Soufflé

Balsamic Green Beans

Sautéed Broccoli Rabe

Stewed Swiss Chard

Fried Green Tomatoes

Zucchini Pancakes

Classic Potato Salad

Creamy Coleslaw

Kevin's Caesar Salad

Tomato and Goat Cheese Tart

Onion Tart

How to Freeze Seafood

How and When to Rinse Seafood

These are some of my favorite vegetable preparations, and they are particularly well suited to serve with fish. I find, for instance, that strong, tangy greens like Swiss chard and broccoli rabe are the perfect complement to simply cooked seafood, as are the fresh, lively tastes of Balsamic Green Beans (page 167) and Fried Green Tomatoes (page 171).

Creamy Coleslaw (page 176) is a must with Old-Fashioned Fish and Chips (page 113), but it's also a good choice with a meal of steamed crabs. Classic Potato Salad (page 174) is another old standby that is good with grilled fish steaks, fish kebabs, or a dinner of steamed clams.

These recipes will get you through the four seasons of New England with variety and flavor. Remember, for best results, start with vegetables that are in season.

POTATOES ANNA

The bottom layer of this dish becomes the crisp golden top when served. Layers of thinly sliced potatoes almost melt together as they cook, transforming the whole into something much greater than the sum of its parts. For best results, use a cast-iron skillet.

A food processor is the best way to slice the potatoes. If you do this step ahead of time, store the potatoes in a bowl of water in the refrigerator to keep them from turning brown. *Serves 6*

> *4 tablespoons butter (3 tablespoons cut into small bits)*
> *8 cups peeled and thinly sliced (⅛ inch) russet potatoes*
> *Salt and pepper*

➤ Preheat oven to 350 degrees.

➤ Melt 1 tablespoon of the butter in a lightly oiled 10-inch cast-iron skillet (or other heavy, ovenproof skillet) over medium heat. As soon as the butter is hot but not browned, place a thin layer of overlapping potato slices in the skillet. Top the potatoes with a little salt and pepper, and a few bits of butter. Leaving the heat at medium and working quickly, repeat this process until you have used all the potatoes, ending with a topping of a little salt and pepper and bits of butter. You should be able to complete the layering in about 3 minutes, giving the potatoes a total of about 4 minutes on top of the stove; if it takes you longer, turn off the heat under the skillet. This step creates the crisp golden crust.

➤ Place the skillet in the middle of the oven and bake, uncovered, for about 40 minutes, or until the potatoes are completely tender.

➤ When the potatoes are done, remove the skillet from the oven. Place a flat, heat-resistant 12-inch serving plate over the skillet. Wearing oven mitts and holding the serving plate tight against the skillet, carefully invert the skillet. The Potatoes Anna will fall right out onto the plate in one whole cake-like form, revealing a beautiful top of golden potatoes. Allow to sit for about 1 minute, then cut into wedges and serve.

CORN PUDDING

This recipe is the heart of simplicity and a very traditional New England dish. Make it in the summer when fresh corn is at its peak.

Serves 4

> *3 cups fresh corn kernels*
> *2 eggs, beaten*
> *1 cup milk*
> *1 teaspoon sugar*
> *Salt and pepper to taste*

✂ Preheat oven to 350 degrees.

✂ In a blender or food processor combine 1 cup of corn kernels with the rest of the ingredients and pulse until the corn is pureed. Transfer the mixture to a bowl and stir in the rest of the corn by hand. Pour into a buttered baking dish, 9 inches by 13 inches, and bake for 30 to 35 minutes. Remove from the oven, let sit for a minute on a cooling rack, cut into squares, and serve.

Love for the Challenge

Every day's different—there is no monotony for people who really love fishing.

—Phil Schwind, *Cape Cod Fisherman*

SPINACH SOUFFLÉ

This is made with frozen spinach, and goes together quickly in a food processor. The soufflé comes out of the oven puffy and golden, with a bit of a crust on the top and a creamy, airy filling. Feta cheese adds a savory bite.

Serves 6 to 8

Fish flakes in Gloucester, Massachusetts.

Up until the middle of the nineteenth century, salting was the primary method of preserving fish. Acres of land were devoted to the use of drying salted fish on flakes. It was important to keep the fish dry, out of the rain.

After the fish had been salted, it was placed on flakes. The construction of flakes was to allow all possible rays of sun to dry the fish, with northwest winds and direct sun giving the best color.

2 boxes frozen chopped spinach
6 eggs
4 tablespoons butter, melted

½ pound Swiss cheese, grated
½ pound feta cheese, crumbled
¼ teaspoon nutmeg

❧ Preheat oven to 350 degrees.

❧ Cook the spinach according to the directions on the package. Transfer to a colander and allow to drain, then wrap in paper towels and squeeze out all the water. Return the spinach to the colander and set aside.

❧ In a large bowl or a food processor fitted with the metal blade, beat the eggs well. Add the butter, cheeses, and nutmeg, and mix thoroughly. Add the spinach and blend in completely.

❧ Spoon the mixture into a buttered baking dish, 9 inches by 13 inches, and bake for 30 minutes. Cut into squares and serve immediately.

BALSAMIC GREEN BEANS

This recipe may change your mind about green beans, which are all too often served soggy and sodden.

Serves 4 to 6

2 pounds fresh green beans, washed
but not trimmed
1 tablespoon olive oil
2 tablespoons minced shallots

1 clove garlic, pressed
2 tablespoons balsamic vinegar
Salt and pepper to taste

❧ Bring a large pot of lightly salted fresh cold water to a boil over high heat. Add the beans and return to a boil. Cook the beans, uncovered, for exactly 3 minutes, no longer. Immediately drain in a colander and place the colander under cold running water, or plunge it into a bowl of ice water, to stop the cooking. Set the cooled beans aside in the colander to drain.

❧ Remove the stem ends of the beans and the strings, if there are any, and cut the beans in thirds (each piece will be a little over an inch long). Lay the cut beans on paper towels while you continue with the recipe.

❧ In a large, heavy skillet heat the olive oil over medium heat. When it is hot, add the shallots and cook until tender but not browned. Add the garlic, stir, and cook until the garlic is fragrant but not browned. Add the green beans, toss lightly, and continue cooking for about 3 minutes, until the beans are hot throughout. Add the balsamic vinegar to the pan, toss quickly, and remove from the heat. Season to taste with salt and pepper, and serve immediately.

How to Freeze Seafood

Most seafood can be frozen without detriment to its taste or texture if cared for properly. Wrap it well first in wax paper or plastic wrap and then in heavy-duty foil, pressing out any air pockets as you go. Fold and seal the edges of the foil securely. Label the package with the contents, their weight, and the date. Then place the package in an airtight plastic freezer bag, seal, and store. (This last step helps prevent freezer burn and keeps fish odors from invading the ice cubes, ice cream, and other items in your freezer.)

When you are ready to use it, remove the wrapping and place the frozen block of seafood on a wide glass plate (a pie plate is good for this). Cover and let sit in your refrigerator overnight or for one day. It should be defrosted and ready for use. The microwave is not a good way to defrost frozen seafood; even on low settings it can cook the edges and dry the fish.

For best results use fish within a month of freezing it.

SAUTÉED BROCCOLI RABE

If you've never had broccoli rabe, the best way I can describe the flavor is a cross between broccoli and spinach. It is tangy and delicious and very high in vitamin C. Wonderful with seafood.

Serves 4 to 6

> *2 pounds fresh broccoli rabe*
> *2 tablespoons olive oil*
> *2 cloves garlic, pressed*
> *2 tablespoons fresh lemon juice*
> *Freshly ground black pepper to taste*

⨾ Clean the broccoli rabe under cold running water, removing any tough stem ends and leaves that are yellowed. Bring a large pot of lightly salted cold water to a boil. Add the broccoli rabe, and when the water returns to a boil, cook, uncovered, for 3 minutes. Drain in a colander and place under cold running water, or plunge it into a bowl of ice water, to stop the cooking. Set the cooled broccoli rabe aside in the colander to drain.

⨾ Heat the olive oil in a large, heavy skillet over medium heat. Add the garlic, stir, and cook briefly, until just fragrant. Add the broccoli rabe and stir to coat it thoroughly with the oil. Cook over medium heat, tossing the broccoli rabe occasionally, for about 4 minutes, or until it is tender but not soft. Add the lemon juice, toss, and remove the pan from the heat. Top with a generous grind of pepper, toss, and serve immediately.

STEWED SWISS CHARD

Swiss chard, like all the dark green leafy vegetables, is a nutritional powerhouse. It is tangy yet smooth in taste, and its rich green color is a lively contrast to seafood that is mostly pale.

Chard is easy to grow and an attractive addition to the garden. If you have the space, put in a short row; you'll be well rewarded.

It is important to the success of this recipe to dice and mince the vegetables extremely small; they are for flavor, and their texture should be hardly apparent.

Serves 4

10 cups tightly packed cleaned chard	*2 cloves garlic, minced*
2 tablespoons olive oil	*½ cup tomato sauce*
⅓ cup finely diced carrot	*½ cup dry red wine*
⅓ cup finely diced onion	*(Cabernet Sauvignon is good)*

Remove and discard any tough stems and ribs from the chard (or save them for a vegetable stock). Wash the chard as you would lettuce and spin dry in a lettuce spinner or spread on paper towels and pat dry. Tear into large pieces and set aside.

Place the olive oil in a large, heavy skillet over medium heat. When hot, add the carrot and onion, and cook, stirring occasionally, until soft and tender but not browned. Add the garlic and continue to cook, stirring, just until the garlic is fragrant—do not allow the garlic to brown. Add the tomato sauce and wine, and bring to a simmer. Stir and simmer over medium-high heat for a few minutes, then add the chard and cover the skillet with a tight-fitting lid. Turn the heat to the lowest setting and cook for 3 minutes. Raise the lid, stir the chard, and cover; cook for another 10 minutes. Remove the lid and continue cooking, uncovered, for 3 to 5 minutes to allow some of the liquid to evaporate. Stir the chard one last time and serve hot.

FRIED GREEN TOMATOES

These are wonderful—crisp on the outside, juicy and tangy on the inside—and great with fish. If you grow your own tomatoes, you can prepare this from the time tomatoes start ripening until well into the fall. Or ask your greengrocer to get you some if there aren't any for sale with the red tomatoes.

I like to use a green tomato that has just the faintest beginning of an orange blush on it. These are more flavorful and juicy than the solid green ones.

Serves 4 to 6

6 large green tomatoes	*½ teaspoon salt*
1 cup buttermilk	*½ teaspoon freshly ground black pepper*
¼ cup unbleached flour	*1 tablespoon (or more as needed)*
⅔ cup yellow cornmeal	*vegetable oil or bacon fat*

➣ Slice the tomatoes ¼ inch to ⅜ inch thick. Set aside on a plate.

➣ Pour the buttermilk into a wide, shallow bowl. In a separate bowl combine the flour, cornmeal, salt, and pepper. Working with 1 tomato slice at a time, dip each into the flour mixture, then the buttermilk, and then the flour again, pressing to coat the slice well. Set them in a single layer on a large platter until you are finished.

➣ Heat the oil or bacon fat in a large, heavy skillet (cast iron is best) over medium heat. When the oil is hot, carefully place some tomatoes without crowding the pan and cook until golden on both sides, turning once with a spatula. As they are cooked, transfer to a platter or cookie sheet covered with brown paper and set in a warm oven with the heat off. Repeat until all the slices are cooked. If necessary, add additional vegetable oil or bacon fat to the skillet as the batches require. Serve immediately.

How and When to Rinse Seafood

Before you begin preparing a recipe with shellfish that you have purchased shucked, such as scallops or clams, check the seafood for grit and shell fragments. One of the best ways to do this is with a quick rinse in salt water: Fill a large glass mixing bowl with fresh cold water and add 4 tablespoons of salt for every quart of water. Stir well. Place the seafood in the salted water and gently swirl with your hands. Quickly and carefully remove the seafood to a clean linen towel or double layer of paper towels set over a rack; gently pat dry.

If you will be using the liquid the shellfish was packed in, such as oysters or clams, strain it before use through a fine-mesh sieve lined with a double layer of dampened cheesecloth.

The other occasion to consider giving fish a "bath" is when seafood that *should* be fresh is smelly. This can happen with improper storage. Before you toss it out, see if it can be salvaged with a rinse. Follow the steps listed above; if the seafood still has an unpleasant odor, you must discard it. Often, however, the bad smell will go away, and the fish will be almost odorless, as truly fresh seafood is.

ZUCCHINI PANCAKES

These little pancakes are tender and savory, and a great way to use up some zucchini if your garden is being overrun by it. Try them with any grilled or baked fish, wedges of garden ripe tomatoes, and a dollop of sour cream.

Serves 4 to 6 (makes about a dozen)

4 cups grated unpeeled zucchini

½ teaspoon salt

4 eggs

1 cup crumbled feta cheese

½ cup chopped onion

1 tablespoon chopped fresh basil

1 teaspoon chopped fresh parsley

1 teaspoon fresh lemon juice

¼ teaspoon freshly ground black pepper

⅓ cup flour

1 tablespoon (or more as needed) olive oil

Place the grated zucchini in a colander set in a bowl. Sprinkle with salt and toss lightly with your hands. Let sit for 15 minutes, then press with your hand until no more liquid drains. Wrap the zucchini in paper towels and squeeze well; more liquid will drain. When the zucchini is completely dry, return it to the colander and set aside.

Beat the eggs well in a large bowl. Stir in the feta cheese, onion, basil, parsley, lemon juice, and pepper. Sprinkle the flour into the mixture and combine well. Add the zucchini and stir until all the ingredients are thoroughly combined.

Heat the oil in a large, heavy skillet over medium heat. When the oil is hot, drop the batter by spoonfuls into the hot skillet without crowding. (Two generous tablespoons of batter makes a nice size pancake.) Cook the pancakes over medium heat, turning only once, until golden on both sides. If you are cooking them in batches, transfer the cooked pancakes to a warm platter. Serve hot, with lemon wedges and sour cream.

Note: It's time to flip the pancakes when little bubbles form in the top of the uncooked side, indicating that the bottom is done. When you flip it, the bottom should be golden. Give the second side slightly less time to cook than the first side. Do one as a tester, cutting into it to check the center if you are unsure.

The Oldest Profession

Fishing is probably the earliest form of hunting, and, as men were surely hunters before they were cultivators, it is actually the oldest industry in the world.

CLASSIC POTATO SALAD

This is my version of the potato salad my parents taught me to make. I offer it here with two dressing choices: a traditional mayonnaise dressing and a warm bacon vinaigrette. If you are going to use the mayonnaise dressing, this can be made up to a day in advance; the salad will improve if it is allowed to sit for at least a couple of hours before serving. The warm vinaigrette dressing gives the salad an entirely different effect.
Serves 6

For the salad:

*2½ to 3 pounds russet or red-skinned
    potatoes, washed and quartered*
¼ cup chopped red onion
½ cup chopped celery

1 cup sliced and quartered cucumber
½ cup chopped gherkins
¼ cup chopped fresh flat-leaf parsley
2 tablespoons chopped fresh basil or dill

For the mayonnaise dressing:

1 cup mayonnaise
1 tablespoon fresh lemon juice
1 teaspoon Dijon mustard
Salt and pepper to taste

For the vinaigrette dressing:

5 slices bacon
⅓ cup olive oil
1 teaspoon Dijon mustard

⅓ cup cider vinegar
1 teaspoon sugar
Salt and pepper to taste

To make the salad:

➤ Cook the potatoes, covered, in a steamer set over boiling water for about 10 minutes, or until completely cooked but not mushy. Set aside to cool.

❧ Peel the cooled potatoes (unless they are very tender red-skinned potatoes) and cut into bite-size chunks. In a large bowl toss together the potatoes, onion, celery, cucumber, gherkins, and herbs. Toss with the mayonnaise or vinaigrette dressing.

To make the mayonnaise dressing:

❧ In a small bowl whisk together the mayonnaise, lemon juice, and mustard. Season to taste with salt and pepper. Pour over the salad and toss to coat thoroughly. Cover the bowl tightly with plastic wrap and refrigerate until ready to serve. Allow the salad to sit at room temperature for 10 minutes before serving if you have chilled it.

Sorting fish on deck, 1980s.

Commercial fishermen spend much of their time at sea sorting the fish they catch—standing, kneeling, and working with both hands—while the boat rolls and heaves.

To make the vinaigrette dressing:

⁂ Cook the bacon in a skillet until it is crisp. Remove from the pan and transfer to paper towels or brown paper. Add the olive oil, mustard, vinegar, and sugar to the pan with the bacon fat and bring to a simmer. Stir until the sugar is dissolved. Remove from the heat and season to taste with salt and pepper.

⁂ Crumble the bacon and add to the salad ingredients. Pour the warm dressing over the salad and toss gently to coat evenly. Serve immediately.

CREAMY COLESLAW

Coleslaw is a must with fish and chips, but it is also a good choice with lots of other seafood meals, including grilled lobster salad rolls, panfried flounder, or broiled mackerel, to name just a few. Make this at least one hour before you plan on serving it.

Serves 6

6 cups shredded green cabbage
2 cups shredded red cabbage
1 cup grated carrot
1 cup mayonnaise

¼ cup white or cider vinegar
1 tablespoon sugar
1 teaspoon Dijon mustard
Salt and pepper to taste

⁂ In a large bowl toss the cabbages and carrot together until evenly mixed.

⁂ In a small bowl whisk together the mayonnaise, vinegar, sugar, and mustard. Season with salt and pepper.

⁂ Pour the dressing over the vegetable mixture and toss gently until all is evenly coated with the dressing. Cover the bowl tightly with plastic wrap. Refrigerate for at least 1 hour, or up to 6 hours, before serving.

KEVIN'S CAESAR SALAD

This is one of my husband's signature dishes. It's great all alone or with just about anything you want to serve with it.

Serves 4

> 1 large head romaine lettuce
> 6 flat anchovy fillets, drained and cut in half
> ⅔ cup Parmesan cheese
> 1 cup Garlic Croutons (page 208)

Dressing:

> 2 cloves garlic
> 6 flat anchovy fillets, drained
> ½ teaspoon Worcestershire sauce
> 2 eggs (see Note)
>
> 4 tablespoons fresh lemon juice
> ⅔ cup olive oil
> Freshly ground pepper to taste
> Salt to taste

➤ Trim and wash the lettuce and spin dry. Tear the leaves into large pieces, wrap in barely dampened paper towels, and set aside.

➤ To make the dressing: Using a mortar and pestle, mix together the garlic and anchovies.

➤ Transfer the paste to a bowl, add the Worcestershire sauce, and stir. Set aside.

➤ In a small bowl beat the eggs with the lemon juice. Allow to sit for 5 minutes, then beat again. Add the anchovy mixture and olive oil to the eggs and whisk together well. Add some freshly ground pepper and a pinch of salt.

➤ Place the lettuce in a salad bowl. Add the anchovy fillets to the lettuce and toss.

➤ Pour the finished dressing over the lettuce and toss to coat well. Sprinkle in the Parmesan cheese and toss again. Add the croutons, toss, and serve.

Note: Use pasteurized eggs if you are concerned about using raw eggs.

TOMATO AND GOAT CHEESE TART

The top of this handsome tart is covered with overlapping slices of tomato, with little bits of the creamy filling showing here and there. Parmesan cheese adds a wonderful bite to the crust, and fresh basil flavors the goat cheese filling.

The pastry for the crust can be made up to a day in advance.

If you've never made a tart, refer to page 203.

Makes one 9-inch tart

*1 Basic Piecrust with Parmesan cheese
  added and blind-baked (see page 202)*
3 large ripe tomatoes
1 cup loosely packed fresh basil leaves
½ cup ricotta cheese

2 eggs
10 ounces goat cheese
Pinch of salt and pepper
1 tablespoon extra-virgin olive oil

➤ Prepare the piecrust.

➤ Slice the tomatoes, horizontally, approximately ¼ inch thick. Salt each slice lightly and lay out on paper towels. Cover with another layer of paper towels and let drain for at least 10 minutes.

➤ Place the basil, ricotta cheese, eggs, goat cheese, salt, and pepper in the bowl of a food processor fitted with the metal blade. Process until well combined (the basil will be finely chopped).

➤ Place the tart pan (lined with the pastry shell) on a cookie sheet. Spoon the filling into the tart shell. Place in a 350-degree oven and bake for 10 to 15 minutes, or until the filling has formed a slightly firm top. Carefully remove from the oven and lay the tomato slices in overlapping rings over the top of the filling. Brush the tomatoes with olive oil and return to the oven to bake for an additional 30 minutes, or until the filling is completely set and the crust is golden. Remove from the oven and cool on a rack.

➤ Serve the tart at room temperature.

ONION TART

This tart is filled with onion slices that have first been wilted with a little olive oil and white wine, and it is held together with a creamy custard. You can make it early in the day and have one less thing to do at dinnertime.

Makes one 9-inch tart

1 Basic Piecrust with Parmesan cheese added and blind-baked (see page 202)	*1 cup dry white wine*
	1 egg
2 tablespoons olive oil	*½ cup sour cream*
4 cups onion slices (Vidalia, Walla Walla, or yellow)	*Salt and pepper to taste*

≫ Prepare the pastry shell.

≫ Heat the olive oil in a large, heavy skillet over medium heat. Add the onion slices and toss gently to coat with oil. Turn the heat to the lowest setting, cover the skillet, and cook the onions for about 10 minutes, occasionally lifting the lid to stir. Add the wine and continue to cook over the lowest heat, uncovered, until the wine is evaporated. Transfer the onions to a bowl and set aside to cool.

≫ In a bowl beat the egg, sour cream, salt, and pepper together well. Pour over the cooled onions and toss to combine evenly. Spoon into the blind-baked tart shell.

≫ Bake in a 375-degree oven for 35 to 45 minutes, until the crust is completely golden and the filling is set with a golden top. Transfer to a rack to cool. Serve at room temperature.

9

Desserts

The next generation.

The lure of boats and the waterfront is too hard to resist, despite many determined parents' plans to the contrary.

Lemon Sorbet

Blueberry-Orange Sorbet

Nut Crisps

Lemon-Soaked Lemon Cake

Melon with Mint Sauce

Baked Pears

Gingerbread with Lemon Sauce

Blueberry-Lemon Sponge Pie
Sorbet

Light desserts, fruit desserts, and lemony desserts make the best end to a seafood meal.

Sorbets are light and refreshing frozen combinations of fruit, fruit juice, and sugar syrup with a texture similar to sherbet. They make a pretty presentation and are considered quite elegant, but as you'll see, sorbets are easy to make.

Thin cookies or plain lemon cake makes a nice partner with a sorbet or simple fruit dessert, and so I include two such recipes here.

You'll also find one hot and one cold fruit dessert, a spicy gingerbread, and, of course, a New England blueberry pie.

LEMON SORBET

This is the quintessential dessert to end a seafood meal—lemony, light, and refreshing. I like to infuse the sugar syrup with sprigs of fresh lemon verbena or mint (both hardy herbs here in New England), but they are not necessary.

Serves 4 to 6

    1 cup water

    1 cup sugar

    ¼ cup loosely packed fresh lemon
      verbena or mint leaves (optional)

    ¾ cup fresh lemon juice

    1 teaspoon grated lemon zest

✒ Combine the water and sugar in a saucepan over medium heat. Add the herbs, if desired. Stir and bring the mixture to a boil. Lower the heat and simmer for 5 minutes. Using a slotted spoon or strainer, remove and discard the herbs. Place the syrup in the refrigerator for at least 2 hours, or until well chilled.

✒ Remove from the refrigerator and stir in the lemon juice and zest. Place in a shallow metal pan, cover with foil, and freeze overnight. Before serving, break the sorbet into chunks and place in a food processor. Process quickly, pulsing, until you have the consistency you want. If the sorbet is now too soft, return it to the freezer for about 10 minutes. Serve in footed glass dishes.

Sorbet

Sorbet makes a wonderful dessert all by itself, but it also can be used as a topping for fresh summer fruit—peaches, nectarines, grapes, melons, or berries.

Sorbet can be flavored with herbs and spices, wines and liqueurs, and countless combinations of fruit. If you want to try inventing some of your own, remember these two rules: Too much sugar can inhibit freezing, as can alcohol; and use seasonal fruit at its peak—a flavorless fruit will produce a flavorless sorbet.

BLUEBERRY-ORANGE SORBET

Make this when blueberries are in season. Serve with Nut Crisps (page 186).
Serves 4 to 6

> ½ *cup water*
> ¾ *cup sugar*
> 4 *cups fresh blueberries*
> ½ *cup fresh orange juice*

⤜ In a small saucepan combine the water and sugar, and bring to a boil. Lower the heat and simmer for 5 minutes. Cover and refrigerate for at least 2 hours, or until well chilled.

⤜ Puree the blueberries and orange juice in a food processor or blender. Pour the mixture through a fine-mesh sieve to remove any solids. Cover and chill for 30 minutes.

⤜ Combine the sugar syrup and pureed blueberry mixture. Place in a shallow metal pan, cover with foil, and freeze overnight. Before serving, break the sorbet into chunks and process briefly in a food processor, pulsing until the desired consistency is achieved. If the sorbet is now too soft, return it to the freezer for about 10 minutes. Serve in footed glass dishes.

NUT CRISPS

These thin, buttery cookies are perfect alongside dishes of fruit sorbet. They are baked in the manner of bar cookies and then scored into squares when the pan comes out of the oven.
Makes about 24 cookies

1 cup (16 tablespoons) butter, softened   *2 cups sifted unbleached flour*
1 cup sugar   *1 cup chopped nuts (pecans, walnuts,*
1 egg, separated   *or almonds)*
1 teaspoon vanilla extract

❞ Preheat oven to 375 degrees.

❞ Cream together the butter and sugar until smooth and light. Beat in the egg yolk and vanilla extract. Add the flour and mix until it is incorporated. Pat the dough evenly into a greased jellyroll pan 9 inches by 15 inches.

❞ Beat the egg white with a fork. Brush it over the top of the dough. Sprinkle the nuts on evenly and gently press them into the dough, using your hands or a rolling pin.

❞ Bake for 15 to 18 minutes, until golden. Place the pan on a cooling rack and let sit for 10 minutes. Using a sharp knife cut into bars. Allow the cookies to cool completely before removing from the pan. Store in an airtight container.

LEMON-SOAKED LEMON CAKE

This cake is baked in a bread loaf pan, soaked with a lemon glaze when it comes out of the oven, and then sliced like bread to serve with fruit desserts. Simple and delicious.
Makes 1 loaf, 5 inches by 9 inches

Cake:

8 tablespoons butter

1 cup sugar

2 eggs, beaten

1¼ cups sifted unbleached flour

1 teaspoon baking powder

¼ teaspoon salt

½ cup milk

½ cup finely chopped almonds

1 teaspoon grated lemon zest

Glaze:

2 tablespoons sugar

Juice of 1 lemon

➥ Preheat oven to 350 degrees.

➥ Cream together the butter and sugar until smooth and light. Beat in the eggs. In a separate bowl combine the flour, baking powder, and salt. Alternately add the flour mixture and the milk to the butter/sugar mixture, beating after each addition. Add the nuts and lemon zest, and blend thoroughly.

➥ Pour the batter into a greased loaf pan 5 inches by 9 inches. Bake for 35 to 45 minutes.

➥ Just before the cake is due to come out of the oven, combine the sugar and lemon juice for the glaze. When the cake is done, transfer the pan to a cooling rack. Using a toothpick poke holes over the top of the cake. Stir the glaze well and pour it evenly over the cake. Let the cake sit in the pan for 10 minutes, then carefully turn it out of the pan to cool completely on the rack. When cooled, wrap in plastic wrap and chill before slicing.

MELON WITH MINT SAUCE

This refreshing dessert is a combination of beautiful shades of cool green. The list of ingredients appears deceptively plain, but don't be fooled: This is another dish where the whole is greater than the sum of its parts.

Serves 4

1 large ripe honeydew melon
2 cups sweet green grapes, seedless
Juice of 2 oranges
Juice of 1 lemon

1 tablespoon finely chopped fresh
  mint
2 tablespoons sugar
Sprigs of mint for garnish

Halve the melon and remove the seeds. Using a melon ball scoop, place the melon balls in a large bowl. Be sure to squeeze the rinds over the bowl of melon balls when all the melon has been removed; there is usually some juice clinging there.

Halve the grapes lengthwise and add to the melon. In a small bowl combine the juices, mint, and sugar. Pour over the fruit and toss gently with a spoon. Cover the bowl tightly with plastic wrap and refrigerate for at least 1 hour to allow the flavors to develop.

Allow the bowl to sit at room temperature for 5 minutes before serving. Toss the fruit gently and serve in footed glass dishes, topped with a sprig of mint.

BAKED PEARS

This simple preparation yields exquisite results. You can assemble the dish in advance and keep it in the refrigerator until you are ready to bake it.

Serves 4

4 ripe Anjou pears, halved, cored
  and peeled
½ teaspoon cinnamon
¼ teaspoon nutmeg
4 tablespoons butter, softened

4 tablespoons brown sugar
1 tablespoon fresh lemon juice
Whipped cream or frozen vanilla
  yogurt for topping

Preheat oven to 350 degrees.

Place the pears in a greased pie plate, arranged like the spokes of a wheel with the narrow ends pointed toward the center, cored surface facing up.

⨾⊃ In a small bowl combine the other ingredients thoroughly. Cover and chill for about 15 minutes, or until the mixture is a thick paste.

⨾⊃ Dividing the mixture evenly among the pears, fill each cavity created by the cores. Spread the rest over the remaining surface of the pears.

⨾⊃ Bake for 20 minutes. Serve warm, topped with whipped cream or frozen vanilla yogurt.

"He pared buckets of potatoes, . . . chopped cabbage, baked huge loaves of bread, . . . pies, cookies, and cakes . . ."

The cook has always been a valuable member of a fishing crew, responsible for feeding the men and, in the case of the fishing schooners, handling the boat while the rest of the men fish. Because of this added responsibility, a good cook was paid a larger share than the rest of the crew. Flo Mills was one of the most famous cooks in the days of the Gloucester fishing schooners:

> Three times a day he prepared food for seventeen men. . . . Flo Mills kept the pot boiling on the ship. He pared buckets of potatoes, sliced turnips, chopped cabbage, baked huge loaves of bread, cooked meat, baked pies, cookies, and cakes, made puddings and doughnuts, and served seventeen dishes of oatmeal each morning, with coffee too. . . .
>
> He kept the ship in the vicinity of the seine boat; he avoided collisions with other schooners . . . tacked and turned the Yosemite with as great facility as if he were handling a sloop in Penobscot Bay . . . sprinting forward to trim the jibs and foresail sheet, darting down to the fo'c'sle . . . to catch a glimpse of a pie in the oven or a boiling pot, and at last picking up the seine boat without upsetting the boat or tearing the seine.
>
> —Raymond McFarland, *The Masts of Gloucester*

Port of Galilee—Narragansett, Rhode Island, 1935.

This port has continued to thrive over the years. Today, however, the boats are bigger (and most are steel hull), the piers are new and more numerous, sail power has been replaced by diesel, and the charming wooden barrels have been replaced by heavy-duty plastic ones.

GINGERBREAD WITH LEMON SAUCE

This is a dense, spicy gingerbread. It's great on its own, but topped with a generous ladle of warm lemon sauce it takes on a second life. Make the sauce while the gingerbread is in the oven.

Serves 6

For the gingerbread:

8 tablespoons butter, softened

½ cup sugar

1 egg, beaten

2½ cups unbleached flour

1½ teaspoons baking soda

1 teaspoon cinnamon

1 teaspoon ginger

½ teaspoon ground cloves

¼ teaspoon salt

1 cup molasses

1 cup hot water

Lemon Sauce:

1 cup sugar

2 tablespoons cornstarch

2 cups boiling water

4 tablespoons butter

½ cup fresh lemon juice

1 tablespoon grated lemon zest

To make the gingerbread:

✺ Preheat oven to 350 degrees.

✺ In a large bowl cream together the butter and sugar. Add the egg and beat well. In a separate bowl combine all the dry ingredients, then set aside. In a large measuring cup combine the molasses and hot water. Alternately add the molasses and dry ingredients to the butter/sugar mixture, beating well after each addition.

✺ Spoon the batter into a greased 9-inch springform pan. Bake for 30 to 40 minutes, or until a toothpick inserted in the center comes out clean. Cool on a rack before cutting in wedges. Serve topped with warm lemon sauce.

To make the sauce:

⤳ Combine the sugar and cornstarch in a saucepan. Add the boiling water and mix well. Place over high heat and bring to a boil; cook at a boil for 5 minutes. Remove from the heat and stir in the remaining ingredients. Serve warm over the gingerbread.

BLUEBERRY-LEMON SPONGE PIE

This is an elegant combination of two old-fashioned dishes—blueberry pie and lemon sponge. The blueberry base is gooey and sweet; the lemon sponge top is light and tart. Bake this the same day you plan to serve it.

Makes one 9-inch pie

1 Basic Piecrust, blind-baked	*3 eggs, separated*
(see page 202)	*7 tablespoons superfine sugar*
3 cups fresh blueberries	*¼ cup plus 3 tablespoons fresh lemon juice*
6 tablespoons granulated sugar	*1 tablespoon grated lemon zest*

⤳ Prepare the piecrust.

⤳ Combine the blueberries and granulated sugar in a saucepan. Stir gently with a spoon; do not smash. Place over medium heat and cook just until the blueberries are juicy and bubbling. Set a fine-mesh strainer over a bowl and pour the blueberry mixture into the strainer.

⤳ Beat the egg yolks with 4 tablespoons of superfine sugar until the mixture is pale and thick. Gradually beat in the lemon juice and zest.

⤳ In a glass bowl beat the egg whites (using clean beaters) until soft peaks form. Gradually add the remaining 3 tablespoons of superfine sugar and beat until the whites are glossy.

⤳ Mix one-fourth of the egg whites into the egg yolk/sugar mixture. Carefully fold in the rest of the egg whites, a fourth at a time.

- Preheat oven to 400 degrees.
- Place the blueberries in the baked pie shell. Add 2½ tablespoons of the strained juice.
- Mound the egg white mixture over the blueberries. Gently spread to cover, all the way to the crust.
- Bake for 15 minutes. Cool thoroughly on a rack before slicing.

Safer Boats for Bigger Risks

Fishing boats today are built and equipped to withstand more dangerous conditions than were earlier boats. Automatic bilge pumps and alarms, steel hulls, radar, radio, flares, and cellular telephones all have increased a fisherman's safety. But even as the equipment has evolved, one thing has not changed: the physical reality of being at sea. The seas, as the waves are referred to, can still be walls of water so high that no horizon is visible when the boat is in the bottom of one, and the winds still blow gale force unexpectedly. If anything, fishermen today expose themselves to rougher and potentially more dangerous weather conditions precisely *because* of the capabilities of the new boats.

Breads, Piecrusts, Sauces, and Other Miscellany

Heading home—view from the "office."

A common expression among fishermen: "The worst day fishing still beats the best day working."

Warm homemade bread on the table changes even the simplest supper to something special. The biscuits and corn bread given here are raised with baking powder and baking soda, so they require no rising time before baking. The focaccia is made with yeast and does need to rise for about an hour. But while the dough is rising, you can do something else.

I still remember how as a young girl visiting my Aunt Mabel and Uncle Dennis on their farm in Texas I enjoyed the buttermilk biscuits my aunt made fresh each morning to serve with the eggs. Those biscuits were so delicious! I'd eat mine split and topped with butter and honey, which would quickly melt because the biscuits were hot out of the oven a few feet from the table. Leftover biscuits would be split and filled with ham for lunch. When I was old enough to think about it, I marveled at Mabel's habit of baking from scratch first thing each morning.

Now I do the same thing at home for my family and bed-and-breakfast guests. Everyone is amazed at the fresh biscuits, but they are very easy and quick to make.

Baking bread does take a little practice, but that's really all there is to it. To get the best results use a top-quality flour; I think King Arthur is best.

Most of the other recipes here can be made in advance and stored in the pantry, refrigerator, or freezer.

Piecrust goes together quickly, and if you like, the dough can be made in advance. Wrap it well in plastic wrap and then foil and store in the refrigerator for up to a week or in the freezer.

The herbed mayonnaise will keep for about two weeks in the refrigerator, and you'll find it's handy for uses beyond specific recipes in this book. Try it on sandwiches, as a dip for fresh vegetables, or thinned with lemon juice as a salad dressing.

Pesto freezes well, so make a batch (or a double batch) whenever fresh basil is in abundance, whether from your own garden or the produce section at your market.

You can make the garlic croutons anytime that's convenient; they keep well in an airtight container at room temperature for a couple of weeks. When I'm at my favorite Italian bakery, I always buy an extra loaf of bread just for croutons if my supply is getting low.

One of the secrets to being considered a good cook is simply a matter of having on hand a variety of ingredients. This small group will get you started.

Fish and the Price of Freedom

Cod fishing was the major industry of the New England colonies and became the main source of funding for the American Revolution. Cod was salted, packed in barrels, and shipped to England. Manufactured goods were sent from Europe to the West Indies, and sugar, rum, and molasses were sent to New England. In 1775 the English parliament passed a bill that prohibited the New England colonies from trading directly with foreign countries, and prevented New England vessels from fishing the banks off Newfoundland. This meant ruin to the New England fish-curing industry, and the edict was one of the leading causes of the Revolutionary War.

BUTTERMILK BISCUITS

Make these according to this recipe until you have them down pat. Then you can improvise by adding a little cheese—grated cheddar or Parmesan cheese—and/or snipped fresh chives or other herb of your choice.
Makes 1 dozen

> *3 cups unbleached flour*
> *½ teaspoon salt*
> *1 tablespoon baking powder*
> *8 tablespoons butter, cut in chunks*
> *1 cup buttermilk*

⤛ Preheat oven to 425 degrees.

⤛ Place the flour, salt, and baking powder in a food processor and pulse once to combine.

⤛ Add the butter and pulse until the mixture resembles coarse meal. Add the buttermilk and pulse just until the dough leaves the sides of the bowl.

⤛ Turn the dough out onto a lightly floured board. Flour your hands and knead and pat the dough into a smooth ball. Flatten it slightly with your hands. Dust a rolling pin with flour and, working from the center of the ball and rolling outward, flatten the dough to about a thickness of ¾ inch.

⤛ Cut with a biscuit cutter and place on an ungreased cookie sheet. Bake for 10 to 12 minutes, at which time they should be golden tan on top, have risen, and will pull apart into a perfect top and bottom. A toothpick inserted in the side that comes out clean tells you they are done. Serve hot.

CORN BREAD

For best results bake this in a cast-iron skillet.
Makes one 10-inch round

> *1 cup cornmeal, plus extra for dusting baking pan*
> *½ teaspoon salt*
> *¼ teaspoon baking soda*
> *1 egg*
> *1 cup buttermilk*
> *1 tablespoon melted bacon fat, or oil*

Preheat oven to 450 degrees.

Rub the inside of a 10-inch cast-iron skillet with oil and dust with cornmeal to give a thin, even coat. Place the skillet in the oven while it preheats.

Combine the cornmeal, salt, and baking soda in a large bowl. In a separate bowl beat the egg; add the buttermilk and beat again. Add the wet ingredients to the dry and mix well.

Add the bacon fat or oil and mix thoroughly.

Pour the batter into the hot skillet and bake for 15 to 20 minutes. When done, the top of the corn bread will be golden and crisp, and the sides will have pulled away from the edges of the pan. Cut into wedges and serve immediately.

FOCACCIA

Focaccia is a flat yeasted Italian bread. The top is brushed with olive oil and sprinkled with rosemary before baking. It is wonderful with pasta dishes as well as salads and soups. There is also a recipe for Mussel-Filled Focaccia on page 14.

If you are not sure how to work with yeast, there are a few important things to remember: Make sure the date on the yeast has not expired; otherwise, it might not rise. Dissolve the yeast in warm, not hot, water—about 110 to 115 degrees is what you want. Allow the yeasted dough enough time to rise in a warm, draft-free place—a warming shelf over a stove is perfect, or the top of your refrigerator.

If you don't bake all three loaves at once, you can refrigerate some of the dough, formed in a ball and wrapped in plastic wrap, for a few days to bake later.

Makes enough dough for three 9-inch round loaves

For the dough:

2 packages dry yeast	½ cup vegetable oil
2 cups warm water	1 teaspoon salt
2 tablespoons sugar	5½ cups unbleached white flour
2 tablespoons olive oil	

Topping for 1 focaccia:

1 tablespoon olive oil
¼ teaspoon kosher salt
1 tablespoon fresh rosemary

To make the dough:

In a large bowl dissolve the yeast in the water. Add the sugar, olive oil, vegetable oil, and salt, and stir until the sugar is dissolved. Mix in 3 cups of the flour and beat until the dough begins to leave the sides of the bowl. (The mixing can be done by hand or with an electric mixer.) Add the rest of the flour and mix until the dough is smooth. Cover the bowl with a clean, damp dish towel and transfer to a warm, draft-free place to rise for 45 minutes.

After 45 minutes the dough should have doubled in size. Punch it down, cover again with the damp towel, and allow to rise for another 45 minutes.

Punch down the dough and turn it out onto a lightly floured board. Knead the dough briefly until it is smooth and elastic. Divide the dough into 3 equal portions.

Preheat oven to 375 degrees.

Form one of the dough sections into a ball. Place it on a baking sheet. Flatten the dough until it is a round loaf about 9 inches in diameter. Using your fingertips, make shallow indentations over the top of the dough. Brush the top with the olive oil, then sprinkle with the salt and rosemary. Cover with a large bowl and let sit for 15 minutes. Remove the bowl.

Bake for 25 to 30 minutes, until the crust is golden and crisp. When tapped, the focaccia sounds almost hollow. Allow to cool slightly on a rack before serving. Repeat with the other two portions or refrigerate or freeze.

BASIC PIECRUST

This basic recipe is very good as is, but it can be modified. Add 3 tablespoons of grated Parmesan cheese when making a crust for a main-course dish; add a tablespoon of sugar when it's for a dessert. You can also add small amounts of spices or dried herbs. Always chill the dough for at least 30 minutes before rolling it out.

Blind-baking (directions follow) prevents the crust from becoming soggy when it is filled.

Makes 1 crust to fit a 9-inch pie plate or tart pan

> *1¼ cups unbleached flour*
> *⅛ teaspoon salt*
> *8 tablespoons butter, cut in pieces*
> *1 tablespoon fresh lemon juice*
> *2 or 3 tablespoons cold water*

Place the flour, salt, and butter in a food processor and pulse until the mixture resembles coarse meal. (Or place in a large bowl and cut in the butter using a pastry cutter or 2 knives.) Add the lemon juice and only enough cold water so that the dough stays together when pinched. Form into a ball, wrap in plastic wrap, and refrigerate until ready to use.

When the dough has chilled for at least 30 minutes (or up to 24 hours), roll it out on a lightly floured surface to a thickness of about ⅛ inch and use to line a pie plate or tart pan. Cover with plastic wrap and refrigerate for 30 minutes to 1 hour before either filling and baking, or blind-baking.

Blind-baking a pastry shell:

➣ Preheat the oven to 425 degrees.

➣ Prick the bottom of the crust all over with a fork. Gently place a sheet of foil over the bottom of the chilled dough and weight with ½ cup of dried beans, rice, or pastry weights.

➣ Bake for 15 minutes. Remove the weights and foil and bake for an additional 3 to 5 minutes, or until the crust is a very pale gold. Remove to a cooling rack until you are ready to fill the shell.

Tarts Versus Pies

Unlike pie plates, tart pans are two pieces: a bottom and a fluted side. Tarts are also thinner than pies and do not have a top crust, as some pies do.

When making a tart, always place the tart pan on a cookie sheet before lining it with pastry and filling. That way you have the cookie sheet to hold on to as you put the tart in the oven and take it out. Drape the rolled pastry dough over the pan and loosely fit the dough in place. Trim the excess, leaving a half-inch overhang. Fold the overhang to the inside of the tart pan, creating a double layer of dough at the fluted edge. Gently press the double layer together and into the sides of the pan so that the two layers become sealed and the fluted edge of the pan shapes the dough. The dough will be slightly higher than the top edge of the tart pan. Gently and slowly roll a *long* rolling pin across the top of the tart pan, starting at the center and rolling out, once in each direction. Pull away with your fingers any dough that has been "trimmed" by the rolling pin.

After baking, carefully slide the tart pan off the cookie sheet and onto a cooling rack. When the tart has cooled completely, place your hand under the bottom to lift it up and away from the fluted ring that makes the side of the pan to expose the beautiful fluted edge. Transfer to a serving plate.

HERBED MAYONNAISE

This is made quickly in a blender, and the results are wonderful. Use as a dip for chilled shrimp cocktail or marinated jumbo shrimp hot off the grill. It goes nicely with lots of other seafood too—grilled tuna, monkfish, and swordfish, to name a few.

Make in advance because it needs to chill for a couple of hours. It will keep, refrigerated, for up to two weeks.

Makes about 2 cups

4 cloves garlic, peeled
1 egg plus 2 egg yolks
2 tablespoons fresh lemon juice
1 teaspoon salt
1¼ cups olive oil

1 cup packed fresh herbs: cilantro,
basil, parsley, dill, or a combination
of your choice
¼ teaspoon cumin (optional)

✒ Place the garlic in a blender and process. Add the egg, egg yolks, lemon juice, and salt, and blend well. Slowly pour in the olive oil in a thin stream while the blender is running. Continue blending until the mixture is thick. Add the herbs and cumin, and process thoroughly. Pour into a clean glass jar, cover tightly, and refrigerate for at least 2 hours.

✒ To use as a salad dressing, mix a little lemon juice and/or buttermilk in a portion of the mayonnaise. Thin to desired consistency.

Cilantro Dressing:

1 cup prepared Herbed Mayonnaise (made with cilantro)
1 tablespoon fresh lemon juice
1 tablespoon buttermilk

✒ Whisk together. Use immediately.

BLENDER HOLLANDAISE

This delicious lemony sauce is quickly made in a blender. Add the herb of your choice. The butter must be piping hot, and you should only make this sauce right before using it. *Makes about 1 cup*

3 egg yolks	*¼ teaspoon freshly ground pepper*
3 tablespoons fresh lemon juice	*1 tablespoon chopped fresh herb: dill,*
8 tablespoons butter, melted	*parsley, basil, or tarragon*

Place the egg yolks and lemon juice in a blender and process on high for 2 minutes. The mixture should be pale yellow and greatly increased in volume.

With the blender running, add the piping hot butter in a slow stream. Continue to process until the mixture reaches the desired thickness. Add the pepper and herb of your choice and process briefly. Serve immediately.

Fishing—the Most Dangerous Job

According to the U.S. Bureau of the Census, the Bureau of Labor Statistics, and the Office of Merchant Marine Safety, commercial fishing is the most dangerous occupation in the United States—far more hazardous than coal mining, which is the most dangerous of land occupations.

HERBED TARTAR SAUCE

Use this with fish and chips, panfried scallops, crab cakes, or any seafood of your choice. Great as a spread for sandwiches made from leftover fish. Use your favorite herb.
Makes about 2 cups

1½ cups mayonnaise
2 tablespoons minced shallots
3 tablespoons finely chopped fresh herb:
  basil, tarragon, dill, or parsley

3 tablespoons minced cornichons
1 tablespoon fresh lemon juice
¼ teaspoon paprika

In a small bowl combine all ingredients well. Store in the refrigerator in an airtight container. This keeps for a few days.

BASIC PESTO

Pesto is handy for pizza, pasta, salads, and baked or grilled fish. I make two batches at a time, and store in the refrigerator and freezer in 1-cup portions.
Makes about 2 cups

2½ cups packed fresh basil leaves
4 cloves garlic
1 cup walnuts or pine nuts
¾ cup olive oil

1 cup grated Parmesan cheese
1 tablespoon fresh lemon juice
Salt and pepper to taste

✎ Place the basil, garlic, and nuts in a food processor and pulse until the mix is finely chopped. Add the oil in a stream with the processor on. Add the cheese, lemon juice, and a little salt and pepper. Pulse briefly. Transfer to an airtight container and store in the refrigerator or freezer. This will keep in the refrigerator for a week.

GREEN TOMATO SALSA

If you grow tomatoes, you'll find this refreshing salsa a handy way to use the green ones at the end of the season. Serve this with Salt Cod Cakes (page 115) for a light summer meal. Use in the Monkfish Fajitas (page 134) or with grilled fish steaks, or mix with some sour cream to use as an alternative to tartar sauce.

Makes approximately 2 cups

1⅓ cups chopped green tomatoes
½ cup chopped onion
2 cloves garlic, finely minced
¼ cup chopped fresh cilantro
½ teaspoon honey or sugar

2 tablespoons fresh lime juice
1 to 3 jalapeño peppers (depending
* on your taste), chopped*
Salt and pepper to taste

✎ Combine all ingredients in a bowl, mixing well. For a finer salsa, transfer half of the mixture to a blender and pulse briefly. Return to the rest of the mixture and stir to combine. Store in an airtight container in the refrigerator. Serve slightly chilled.

JOHNNYCAKES

These little griddle cakes, made primarily from white cornmeal, are a traditional New England side dish; they are called for in the Cod with Cider Cream Sauce recipe (page 117), but they are good with all kinds of seafood meals.

Makes about 1 dozen (3-inch diameter)

1 cup johnnycake meal (stone-ground white cornmeal)
1 tablespoon sugar
½ teaspoon salt
1 cup boiling water (or milk for a thinner, crisper johnnycake)

3 to 4 tablespoons milk (but use water if you substitute milk for the boiling water)

In a large bowl combine the cornmeal with the sugar and salt. Add the boiling water and mix well. Stir in the milk; the mixture should be the consistency of thick pancake batter.

Ladle the batter onto a well-oiled hot griddle set over medium heat and cook for 6 minutes per side. The outside should be golden and crisp, and the inside should be smooth and hot. Serve immediately, with butter and salt and pepper.

GARLIC CROUTONS

You'll need these for Caesar salad, of course, and a number of recipes in the Salads chapter. I like to have them on hand to sprinkle in soup.

Makes about 8 cups

1 large loaf Italian bread (12 ounces is standard)
4 tablespoons olive oil
4 tablespoons butter
4 cloves garlic, peeled and scored

✂ Trim the crust off the loaf, slice in ½-inch slices, and cut those into cubes. If the bread is fresh, allow the cubes to sit for half a day to dry out.

✂ In a 12-inch cast-iron skillet heat 2 tablespoons of the oil and 2 tablespoons of the butter over medium heat. Add 2 cloves of garlic. When the oil is hot, add half of the bread cubes, quickly tossing so that all are coated with the oil/butter mixture. Cook the bread over medium heat, tossing often, until it is golden. Transfer to brown paper to drain and cool.

✂ Repeat with the rest of the ingredients.

✂ When the croutons have cooled, discard the garlic and store the croutons in an airtight container. If the croutons are not crisp enough, put them on a large baking pan and place them in a 350-degree oven for about 15 minutes, tossing every 5 minutes.

How to Roast Peppers

Wash the peppers and place them whole, barely touching, on a cookie sheet or in a shallow pan. Set under a hot broiler, 4 to 6 inches from the flame. Turn occassionally with tongs and broil until the skin is completely black.

Place the roasted peppers in a paper bag and allow to cool for a few minutes. When the peppers are cool enough to handle, pinch and lift off the charred skin (it will come away easily), working over a bowl to catch any juices. Discard the skin, then halve and seed the peppers. They are now ready to be used in any recipe that calls for roasted peppers. Some recipes call for the juices as well. These are also good added to salad dressings.

Roasted peppers can be stored in the refrigerator for a day or two before using.

Appendix

Filleters at a Gloucester fish house take a break, 1940s.

The commercial introduction of filleting as a processing method in 1921 and Clarence Birdseye's quick-freezing process later in the 1920s helped make ocean fish available across the nation.

HOW TO FILLET A FISH

Most fish at your local market is available already filleted. But at a good fish market—particularly one near a fishing port—you will also find whole fish on display, such as bluefish, striped bass, mackerel, tautog, and sea trout, depending on the time of year. Knowing how to fillet a whole fish will allow you to choose from a greater variety. You will pay less per pound, and you can use the fish carcass to make fish stock.

These are basic directions and illustrations that will work for *most* fish (working with a flat fish like flounder is slightly different). The more you practice, the better you will become at it.

Filleting a fish

1. Always start with a sharp knife!
2. *Remove the fins:* Using kitchen shears, cut off all the fins except the tail fin. This step is optional—I like to do it to make the fish easier to hold.
3. *Remove the scales:* Hold the fish by the tail, and using a dull knife held at an angle against the skin, scrape toward the head. Do this over the whole body until you can feel with your hands that all the scales are gone and the body is smooth. Work outdoors or in a deep sink because the scales will fly all over the place as they are scraped off.
4. *Clean the fish:* Using the tip of the knife, make an incision from the area under the jaw, along the belly, all the way to the last fin before the tail. Remove and discard the entrails and rinse the fish well under cold running water.
5. *Cut the fillets from the body:* Place the scaled, cleaned fish on a cutting board with the backbone facing you (see top illustration on page 216). Make an incision behind the gills, holding the knife at a slight angle, and cut from the top of the head to the bottom until the knife hits bone. Make a similar cut where the body meets the tail. Next, use the tip of the knife to make an incision in the skin along the backbone, from the back of the head to the tail. Working from the head toward the tail, insert the fillet knife through the incision in the skin, parallel to and along the backbone (see middle illustration on page 216), and toward the belly cavity. Move the knife evenly toward the tail, always keeping the knife cutting just above the bones. When you reach the

tail fin, the knife will automatically cut through the last bit of meat and sever the fillet from the body. You now should have a boneless fillet, with the skin on. Turn the fish over and repeat the process.

6. *Skin the fillet:* Unless you plan to cook the fillet with the skin, place the fillet, skin side down on a cutting board (see bottom illustration on page 216). As close to the tail end as possible, make an incision through the meat down to, but not through, the skin. Grip this bit of meat and skin with one hand and with your other hand hold the knife pressed firmly at a 45-degree angle to the cutting board. Use your hand holding the tail end of the fillet to tug and wiggle the fillet toward the blade of the knife. This motion will cleanly remove the skin from the meat. When you are done, you should have a beautiful skinless fillet. If there are still bits of skin adhering to the fillet, carefully cut them off with the knife. If there are any pin bones in the fillet, remove them by cutting a v-shaped incision to remove them, or pull them out with tweezers. Save the fish parts for stock.

How to Fillet Skate

Skate is a bit difficult to fillet. If at all possible, have your fish market fillet it for you. Most will do this with a little advance notice. Otherwise, do as follows:

Place the skate wing on a wooden cutting board with the dark side down (the dark side has little prickers in the skin, and this will help hold it to the board as you skin it). Using a very sharp knife, slowly and methodically cut the skin away from the meat. Repeat the process on the other side, but wear gardening gloves because the prickly side can cut your hands. You will have a skinned skate wing with a sheet of cartilage separating the two sides (each side is a fillet). You can cut the meat away from the cartilage.

Alternately, you can remove the skin by giving the wing a quick poaching. Place the wing in a pan with just enough water to cover. Bring to a boil, cover, and cook for 2 minutes. Remove from the heat and transfer the skate to a bowl of cold water to stop the cooking. The skin can now be easily lifted or scraped off.

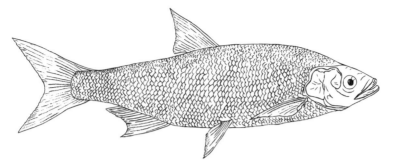

Fish

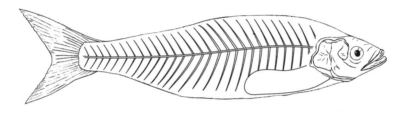

Skeleton and belly

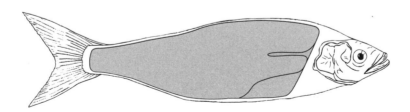

Potential fillet

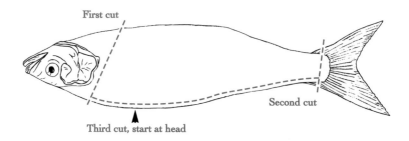

Work with backbone toward you.

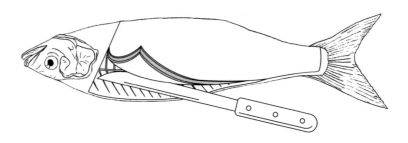

Knife should be almost flat against bone.

Place on cutting board, skin side down.

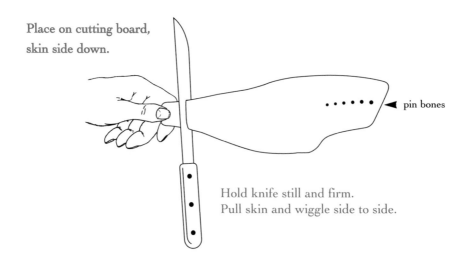

pin bones

Hold knife still and firm.
Pull skin and wiggle side to side.

Purchasing Guide

When buying whole fish, look for clear, bulging eyes and bright red gills.

Fresh fish—whole or fillets—should have hardly any odor at all, and what odor there is should be pleasant. The meat should be firm and elastic, and fillets should be moist and gleaming. Whole fish or fillets should be free from slime.

When you visit a fish market, never hesitate to ask questions. This is a good way to learn more about what's available, what's "in season," and whether its season is about to end or is just beginning.

Nowadays most fish is available year-round because the boats are able to go farther afield and in worse weather than ever before. You will notice, however, that seafood prices change throughout the year: Squid that costs 78 cents a pound whole in November may be going for $1.99 a pound in March. The price of all seafood fluctuates based on supply and demand. The best way to purchase fresh seafood—at its best and for a good price—is to visit your fish market regularly and discover what the season and price cycles are for your area.

Outlaws and Misfits

For the Puritans, fishing was by its nature incompatible with leading a "good" life as taught by the Church because it was not disciplined or regimented work, as farming was.

In addition, life at sea has always presented a way for men to "hide out" from society at large, convenient for outlaws. During whaling times this was literally true, as one of them, Enoch Cloud, recorded in his journal in 1851:

Out of every 100 men in the service [whaling] 75 are run-away apprentices; of the remaining 25, 20 are fugitives from justice—leaving a remainder of 5 honest men!

—Enoch Carter Cloud, *Enoch's Voyage: Life on a Whale Ship*

Seafood and Good Nutrition

Doctors and nutritionists have been advising us for years now to lower the amount of fat in our diets, especially saturated fat (the kind that contributes to heart disease). *All* seafood is very low in saturated fat, and most is low in total fat, as you can see by the chart on page 220. As a comparison, consider the following: a 3-ounce serving of chicken (about half a chicken breast) roasted with the skin on contains about 7 grams of fat; roasted without the skin, about 3 grams of fat. Most shellfish and non-oily seafood—clams, scallops, squid, cod, flounder, monkfish, whiting, and so forth—contain closer to 1 gram of fat per 3-ounce serving.

Although low in fat, seafood is a good source of protein—as high or higher than chicken. And the seafood that has high levels of fat (still nowhere near beef) is high in Omega-3 acids, believed to raise the levels of HDL (good) cholesterol and reduce the risk of heart disease and stroke. The American Medical Association released the results of a series of studies in 1995 showing that eating one serving a week of fish high in Omega-3 fatty acids can reduce the risk of heart attack by 50 percent to 70 percent.

All seafood contains Omega-3 fatty acids, some more than others. It is found in highest concentration in mackerel; herring, salmon, anchovies, tuna, bluefish, striped bass, and swordfish are also good sources. Generally, the oilier or "fattier" the fish, the higher the Omega-3 content.

There's a lot of confusing information about cholesterol floating around these days. And because certain seafood, particularly lobster, shrimp, and squid, contains higher levels, it's important to be able to sort out the facts. Here's what you need to know: The body needs cholesterol to survive. The cholesterol present in food is *not* what causes high cholesterol levels in the body—fat is. Saturated fat is primarily responsible for increasing blood cholesterol, and all seafood is low in saturated fat (the three previously mentioned contain less than 1 gram per serving).

According to the Washington, D.C.-based Center for Science in the Public Interest, seafood represents one of the best choices for a healthy diet. "Bake it, broil it, blacken it, grill it—as long as you don't fry it," said Jayne Hurley, the group's senior nutritionist. The National Fisheries Institute, a seafood trade organization, responded to the Center's findings with agreement except on the warning about fried fish: "Fried items, including fried seafood, can be enjoyed in moderation along with a balanced and sensible diet over the course of several meals or several days."

Seafood is also a good source of many vitamins and minerals, as you can see in the chart that follows.

Unloading the catch, Stonington, Connecticut, 1990s.

The perishability of fresh fish, and fluctuations in its value, combine to challenge fishermen both at sea and ashore.

Nutritional Information Chart

In this chart the values are based on a 3½-ounce or 100-gram portion (a standard nutritional measurement) of uncooked seafood. It is important to note that the "total" fat gram figures *include* the Omega-3 fatty acids; do not add the two together.

		Calories	Protein (grams)	Total Fat (grams)	Omega-3 (grams)	Other Benefits
Bass	Sea	97	18.43	2	.60	181 IU vitamin A 218 mg potassium
	Striped	97	17.73	2.33	.75	3.25 mg B-12
Bluefish		124	20.04	4.24	.77	293 mg potassium
Clams		74	12.77	.97	.14	14 mg iron 96 mg calcium
Cod		82	17.81	.67	.18	342 mg potassium
Crab		87	18.06	1.08	.32	89 mg calcium
Flounder		91	18.84	1.19	.20	1.29 mg B-12 307 mg potassium
Haddock		87	18.91	.72	.19	1.18 mg B-12 339 mg potassium
Halibut		110	20.81	2.29	.40	440 IU vitamin A 9.2 mg niacin
Herring		158	17.96	9.04	1.57	110 IU vitamin A
Lobster		90	18.80	.90	.37	61 mg calcium
Mackerel		205	18.60	13.89	2.30	430 IU vitamin A 2.1 mg iron
Monkfish		76	14.48	1.52	.20	23 mg magnesium
Mussels		86	11.90	2.24	.44	4 mg iron
Oysters		69	7.06	2.47	.44	6.7 mg iron 94 mg calcium 320 IU vitamin A
Salmon		146	21.62	5.95	1.44	7.2 mg niacin 310 IU vitamin A

		Calories	Protein (grams)	Total Fat (grams)	Omega-3 (grams)	Other Benefits
Scallops		88	16.78	.76	.20	26 mg calcium
Sea Trout		104	16.74	3.61	.37	290 mg potassium
Shrimp		106	20.31	1.73	.48	3.1 mg iron
Skate		89	19.60	.70	—	.02 mg B-1
Squid		92	15.58	1.38	.49	200 mg potassium 4 mg vitamin C
Swordfish		121	19.80	4.01	.64	9.7 mg niacin 245 mg potassium 2000 IU vitamin A
Tautog		94	18.75	1.57	.41	22 mg calcium 227 mg potassium
Tilefish		96	17.50	2.31	.43	22 mg calcium 368 mg potassium
Tuna	Bluefin	144	23.33	4.90	1.17	8.01 mg B-12 1856 IU vitamin A 214 mg potassium
	Yellowfin	108	23.38	.95	.22	8.3 mg niacin
Whiting		90	18.31	1.13	.22	60 mg calcium

Photo Credits

Index

Home from cod fishing, 1920s.

"Next Sunday you'll be hirin' a boy to throw water on the windows to make ye go to sleep. . . . Do you know the best of gettin' ashore again?" "Hot bath?" said Harvey. His eyebrows were all white with dried spray. "That's good, but a night-shirt's better. I've been dreamin' o' night-shirts ever since we bent our mainsail. . . . It's home, Harve. It's home! Ye can sense it in the air. We're runnin' into the aidge of a hot wave naow, an' I can smell the bay-berries. Wonder if we'll get in fer supper."

—Rudyard Kipling, *Captains Courageous*